GUITAR TABS MASTERY FOR BEGINNERS

GUITAR TABS MASTERY FOR BEGINNERS

NO-GUESSWORK GUIDE TO READING GUITAR TABS IN UNDER A DAY

PAUL STERLING

First Note™
Beginner to Boss

Copyright © 2025 FirstNote

All rights reserved. No part of this publication may be reproduced, distributed, or transmitted in any form or by any means, including photocopying, recording, or other electronic or mechanical methods, without the prior written permission of the publisher, except in the case of brief quotations embodied in reviews and certain other non-commercial uses permitted by copyright law.

ISBN13: 978-81-989937-8-6 (Ebook Edition)
ISBN13: 978-81-989937-3-1 (Paperback Edition)
ISBN13: 978-81-989937-1-7 (Hardcover Edition)

DEDICATION

To every beginner who's ever felt the thrill of holding a guitar for the first time,
may this book help turn that spark of curiosity into the steady rhythm of confidence.
Your music journey starts with one note.
Make it count.

CLAIM YOUR FREE BONUSES!

THANKS FOR PICKING UP GUITAR TABS MASTERY FOR BEGINNERS! TO HELP YOU GET EVEN FASTER RESULTS, WE'VE INCLUDED A FEW EXCLUSIVE BONUSES - 100% FREE.

Bonus #1:
TABs Cheat Sheet
(Printable PDF)
Quick reference for TAB notation
All key TAB symbols

Bonus #2:
Audio Files
Hear every exercise played correctly
Practice by ear and improve faster

Bonus #3:
Guitar Mastery Starter Kit
(Printable PDF)
Must-have apps, tools & resources
Beginner gear tips
Practice strategies that work

Bonus #4:
FirstNote Newsletter
Monthly tips, lessons & updates
Early access to new books & offers

Download everything at

playfirstnote.com/bonuses

No guesswork. No fluff. Just tools to help you play better - faster.

CONTENTS

INTRODUCTION

HOW GUITAR TABS TURNED ME INTO A ROCK STAR (WELL, ALMOST)

THE PHONE CALL THAT CHANGED EVERYTHING

Picture this: a nervous 19-year-old in baggy shorts and an oversized T-shirt, gripping his mom's old rotary phone like it was a lifeline. My knees were shaking, and my palms were sweaty.

That was me, more than twenty years ago, when one phone call flipped my world upside down.

On the other end was my mentor, the guitarist I admired more than anyone. His playing had always felt alive, like the guitar itself was speaking.

But that day, it wasn't music I heard. It was his voice, cracking.

"Carpal tunnel syndrome," he said. "Doctor's orders: no guitar for three months."

It was crushing news for him, and even worse for the big-name band he was touring with. Their biggest show was in just a week. And then came the real shock:

He asked me to take his place.

A CRAZY PLAN AND A CRAZIER DEADLINE

Me? I was just a bedroom guitarist. I'd spent years playing alone, dodging music theory like it was homework, and performing only for my dog (who cared more about chewing sneakers than listening).

I had never been on stage in my life.

Still, for some reason, he believed in me.

"You've got this," he said, trying to sound optimistic. "You just need to learn 22 songs, solos, and all by next weekend."

No rehearsals. No lessons. Just me, a guitar, and a terrifyingly short countdown.

TABS: THE SECRET WEAPON THAT SAVED ME

I tried learning the first song by ear. Two hours later, I had barely figured out the chorus. At that rate, I'd never survive the set list.

Then I stumbled onto something that changed everything: guitar TABs.

It was a scrappy, fan-made chart I found online. Not pretty, not perfect, but it was a map. Suddenly, I had a way forward.

I locked myself in my room, fueled by chips and soda, and spent five days glued to those TABs. By the end, I played the songs for my mentor, and his jaw dropped. From despair, his face lit up with pride.

That Saturday, I walked on stage in front of 5,000 fans. Did I miss a few notes? Absolutely. Were my knees shaking? Like crazy. But I made it through.

TABs didn't just save me, they launched me.

WHAT'S MY FREAKOUT GOT TO DO WITH YOU?

You might be wondering: *"Okay, cool story. But what does this have to do with me learning guitar?"*

The answer: everything.

TABs were the tool that transformed me from a nervous kid fumbling with chords into a guitarist who could actually play songs people wanted to hear. They gave me confidence, speed, and a way to finally bridge the gap between my dreams and reality.

And they can do the same for you.

I know what it's like to wish you could play your favorite songs, but feel stuck. TABs were my shortcut to making real music, and they can be yours, too.

YOUR GOLDEN TICKET STARTS HERE

Think of guitar TABs as your guitar's instruction manual. They don't replace practice, but they make the journey much faster and a whole lot more fun.

By the end of this book, you'll be able to read TABs and unlock thousands of songs, everything from easy campfire classics to the riffs that made you want to pick up a guitar in the first place.

I'm not here to drown you in music theory or scales. I'm here to show you the same path I stumbled onto, one that can get you playing music quickly, confidently, and with a smile on your face.

So grab your guitar, and let's dive in. The fun starts now.

CHAPTER 1
THE BASICS OF GUITAR TABS
YOUR SHORTCUT TO PLAYING SONGS RIGHT AWAY

GUITAR TABS, ALWAYS AN ACE UP YOUR SLEEVE

When things get tough, the tough turn to TABs. I haven't been that skater boy for a while (I wear normal-size clothes now), but the TAB trick has saved me many times over the years.

Knees steady, dry palms.

It has always been my secret, the ace up my sleeve. I've been to auditions and studio sessions that required knowing songs, and I could just step into the next room and pull out my phone to learn them.

In a way, TAB notation is like a superpower you get to use whenever you need it. You know, like in the movies: *Bam, you go out the door, and Bam, you show up dressed in spandex with your underwear outside your tracksuit.*

Jokes apart, TABs are a highway to you becoming a song encyclopedia. At least, that's what they did with me (so far, I haven't got to wear the superhero suit, but you never know).

WHAT EXACTLY ARE GUITAR TABS?

First things first, what are guitar TABs?

In simple terms, TABs are a way of writing music specifically for the guitar (and other stringed instruments). Instead of traditional sheet music with notes on a staff, TABs use numbers and lines to show you:

- Which **string** to play
- Which **fret** to press
- And the symbols show you when to play techniques like bends, slides, hammer-ons, and much more

Think of them as a guitar-specific alphabet. Instead of learning the entire "language" of music notation, you're learning a shorthand designed just for guitar players.

TABS VS. SHEET MUSIC

You've probably seen sheet music before. It's the standard musical language taught in conservatories and schools. It's incredibly detailed, making it difficult and time-consuming to learn.

Here's how TABs and sheet music differ:

- **Sheet music** works for any instrument. **TABs** are just for stringed, fretted instruments, like the guitar.

- **Sheet music** shows both pitch *and* rhythm / timing. **TABs** focus mainly on pitch (what note / chord to play), and you learn when to play the notes and the rhythm by listening to a song or piece of music.

- **Sheet music** takes years of study. **TABs** can be learned in a day.

Now, don't get me wrong, reading music is an amazing skill, and if you learn it, you'll speak the "universal language" of musicians. But most guitarists just want to pick up their favorite songs and start playing. And that's exactly what TABs make possible.

WHY MORE INFORMATION ISN'T ALWAYS BETTER

You might wonder, "If sheet music shows more, isn't it better?"

Not always. Imagine you're at the grocery store and want to check your bill. Do you really need to use advanced algebra to do it? Of course not, you just need the essentials.

It's the same with guitar. TABs give you exactly what you need, where to put your fingers, and what to play. That's enough to start making real music right away.

THE BEST SHORTCUT TO LEARNING SONGS

One of the fastest ways to learn a new song is by looking up its TAB online. It's much quicker than trying to figure everything out purely by ear.

The best part? You'll usually find several versions of the same song. When a few of them agree, you know you're on the right track. That's a lot better than confidently strumming the wrong chord while the rest of the band is in a different key!

TABs also give your imagination a boost. Have you ever listened to a song and wondered, *"Is the guitarist bending that note? Sliding? Palm muting?"* With TABs, you don't have to guess; it's written right there.

And because guitar TABs are constantly updated by players around the world, they reflect modern techniques. Traditional sheet music has been around for centuries, but TABs keep up with new styles, new tricks, and the way real guitarists actually play.

A SIMPLER WAY

If you ask me, the best option is to learn TABs first. They'll get you playing music quickly and keep you motivated. Then, if you want to go deeper into theory or even use sheet music later on, you'll already have the joy of playing on your side.

In short:

- **Sheet music** is like learning to read ancient hieroglyphics, amazing, but slow.
- **TABs** are like learning to read street signs; you'll actually get where you want to go fast.

And that's why they've been my go-to tool ever since I discovered them.

ENOUGH INFORMATION TO PLAY

So, what do you *really* need to play a song?

Honestly, not much. Just the chords, lyrics, and a few riffs or solos. TABs give you all of that in a clear, visual way.

The first time you strum through a song you love using a TAB, you'll feel it immediately: this is the fast track to playing guitar. No theory exam required.

THE BOTTOM LINE

TABs are the simplest, most effective way to start playing guitar. They're not a "lesser" version of music notation; they're a tool created *for you*, the guitarist, to make learning quicker and more fun.

By the end of this book, you'll not only know how to read them, you'll use them confidently to play real songs. And trust me, that moment when the music finally clicks under your fingers? It's worth every second of practice.

CHAPTER 2

TAB LAYOUT

STRINGS, FRETS, AND SYMBOLS THAT BRING TABS TO LIFE

Before we start having next-level fun playing some of your favorite tunes, let me briefly introduce you to what a guitar TAB looks like. We're going to talk about the fun stuff like bends, tapping, and hammer-ons in a bit, but first things first.

THE SIX LINES = YOUR SIX STRINGS

When you look at a guitar TAB, the very first thing you'll notice is six horizontal lines stacked on top of each other.

Each line represents a string on your guitar:

This is what a TAB looks like:

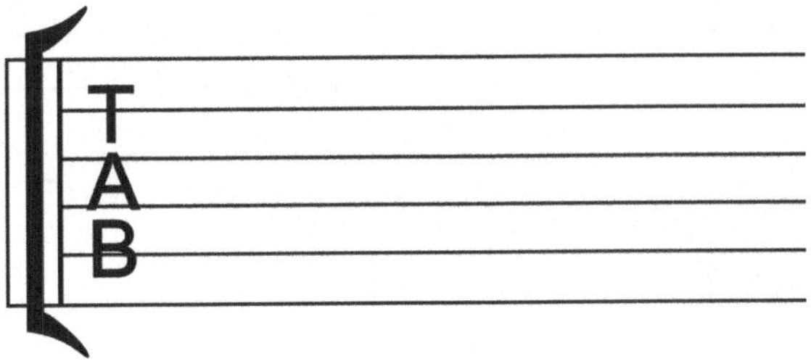

The TAB mirrors your guitar's fretboard.

The **bottom line** is your **low E string** (the thickest one).

The **top line** is your **high e string** (the thinnest one).

• • •

TABs are written as if you're looking down at your guitar on your lap. Therefore, the bottom line of the TAB is the string closest to you, the low E string, while the top line of the TAB is the string farthest away, the high e string.

NUMBERS = FRETS

The lines show strings, and the numbers on them show **frets**:

- A **0** means you play the string **open** (no fingers, just the string).
- A **1 indicates that you should** press a finger down on the **first fret**.
- A **2** means that you need to press your finger down on the **second fret**, and so on.

Simple, right?

The numbers you'll see on each line don't indicate what fingers you should use, as in a chord diagram, but the number of the fret/frets you need to press.

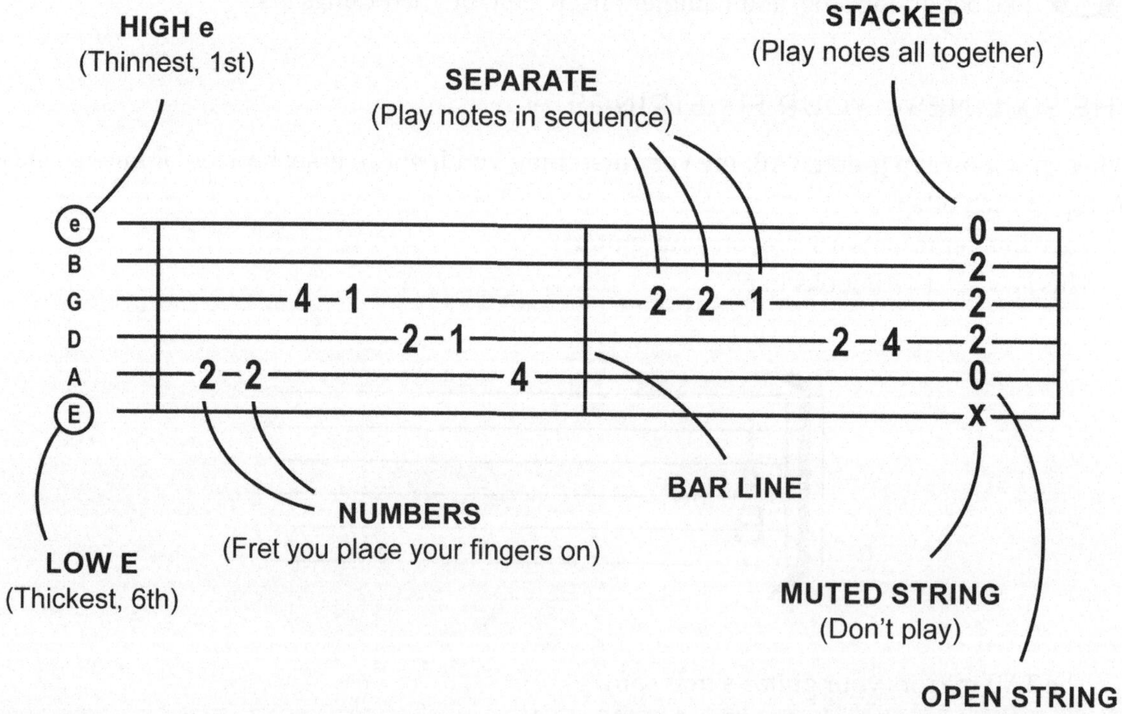

For example, look at the following image and name the chord. A little clue? It's a major chord.

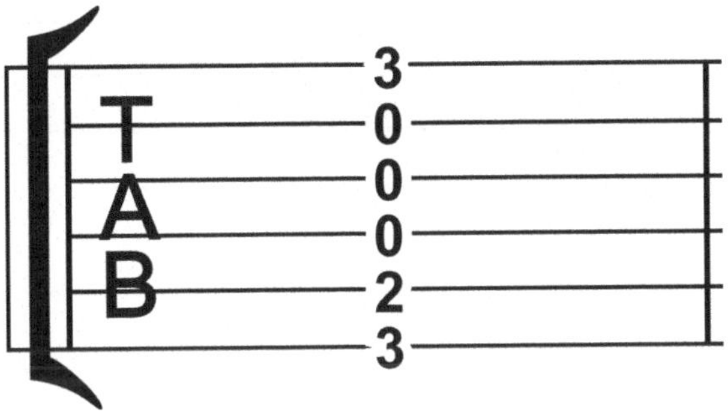

Yes! You're right! It's a G major chord. As you can see, the low G note is on the third fret of the sixth string at the bottom of the TAB, and there is a B note on the second fret of the fifth string.

You might be thinking, "That's cool, but what about those zeros?" while you scratch your head with a half-worn pick. Well, those strings need to be played open and left to ring. As you know, D, G, and B (AKA the fourth, third, and second) strings are part of the G major chord. The chord ends with the high G note on the third fret of the first string.

Now, check out these two examples, these are the D and C chords:

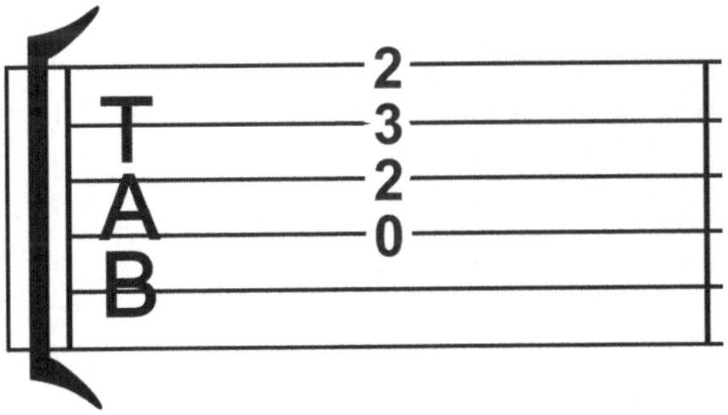

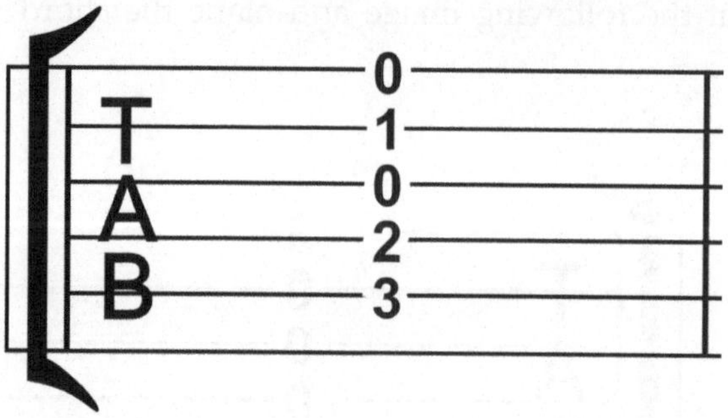

Yeah, I know, some strings don't have numbers! Well, that's because you shouldn't play them. Easy, huh? I know, TABs are cool!

Wait, what about barre chords?! I got you covered on that, too! Check out this F Major chord:

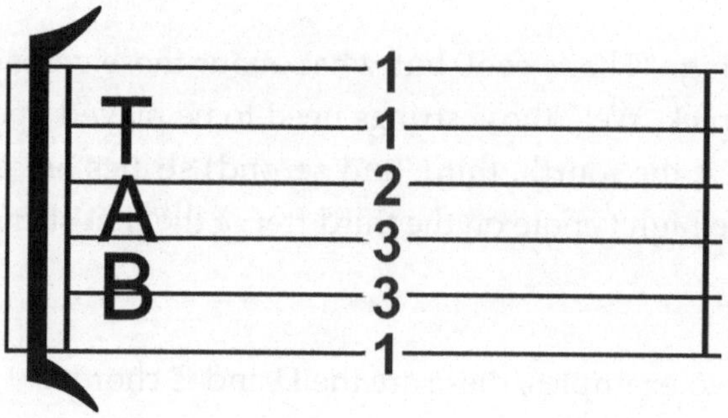

That's exactly how you play chords, reading TABs.

Oh, wait, if you're wondering just how difficult reading music notation is compared to TABs… Can you play this?

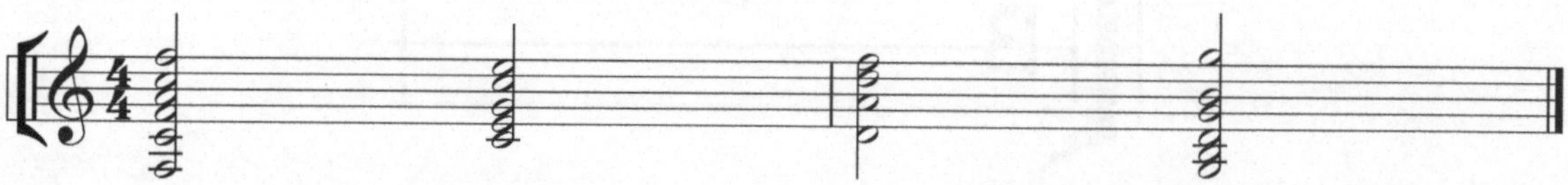

It sure looks intimidating, doesn't it? But let's see what it looks like in TAB; it's a million times easier to quickly read and play.

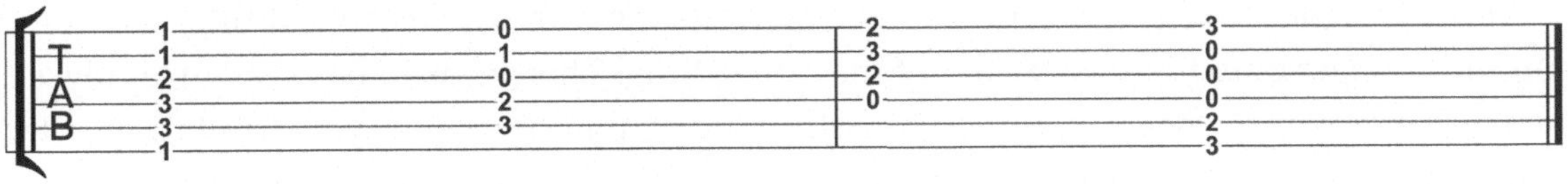

I know, a piece of cake, just follow the numbers and the strings and you're done.

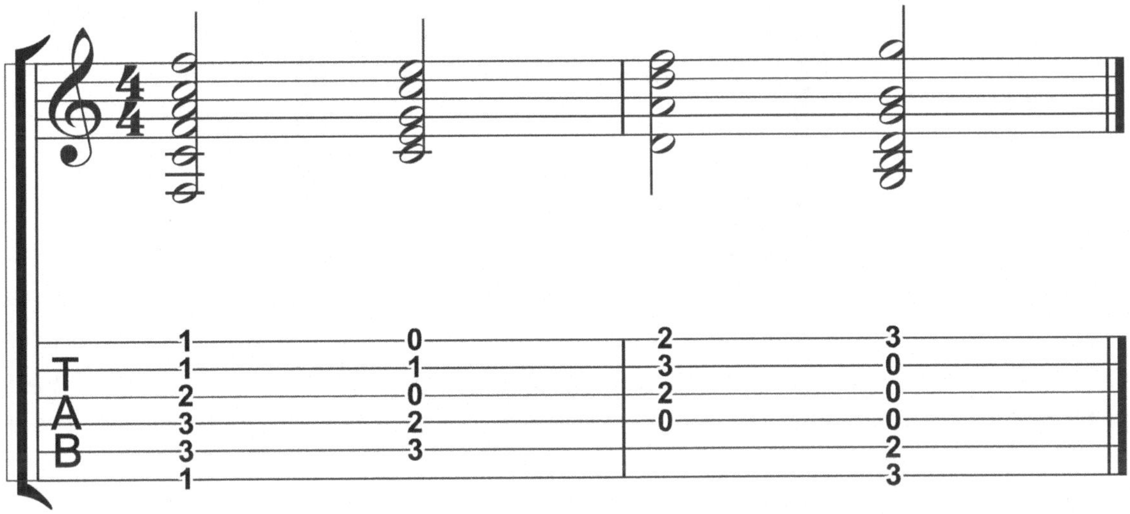

Well, there you go, both are exactly the same chord sequence - F, C, D, and G - I told you, TABs are CO-OL!

BASIC SYMBOLS (MEET THE GANG!)

Now that the chords are clear, it's time to meet your new gang of friends. These symbols are an absolute must to understand riffs, licks, and solos.

They represent those tasty moves we make to transform the guitar into a more expressive, melodic instrument. You know, besides practicing the moves, you need to have the chops.

Take it from someone who went directly from bedroom to stage, those moves in front of the mirror paid off no end!

To download the audio files for the TAB symbols mentioned in this section, head to **playfirstnote.com/bonuses**.

HAMMER-ON (H)

The Hammer-on is a very popular guitar move that's been used by every guitar hero or seasoned player you can think of.

The technique goes like this: play a note, such as the fifth fret of the G string, then press your third finger onto the seventh fret of the same string. This needs to be done forcefully, i.e., hammered down, so that you clearly hear the second note. Perhaps you already knew this technique; if not, check out Jimi Hendrix, he kind of had it figured out a bit (or a lot!).

In TAB, it is shown like this:

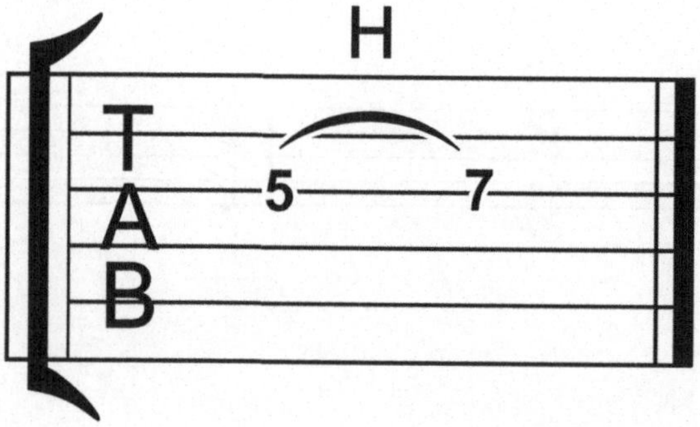

This shows a note played on the fifth fret of the third string (G). The curved line with the H on top means the following note, on the seventh fret of the same string, doesn't need to be picked, but hammered.

The letter 'H' is not always included; sometimes it is only indicated by a curved line.

The Sketchy Version

Those of us who lived through the glorious early days of the internet had to learn many skills, like creating TAB notation using Notepad. So, if you go deep enough in your TAB search, you'll find the Notepad version - a sketchy version (but more often than not, the correct one), and this is how to read it.

```
e|-------------|
B|-------------|
G|--5h7--------|
D|-------------|
A|-------------|
E|-------------|
```

PULL-OFF (P)

Pull-offs are the reverse of hammer-ons. I remember when I learned the technique, I became a pull-off master; I used them in every solo! I don't use them as often these days, but believe me, once you start recognizing the way they sound, you'll hear them everywhere.

How to do a pull-off? Well, you use your fretting finger to pull off (duh!) a note on a particular string to another note on the same string. As with the hammer-on, this will give you two notes from one pick of a string.

It looks like this in TAB notation:

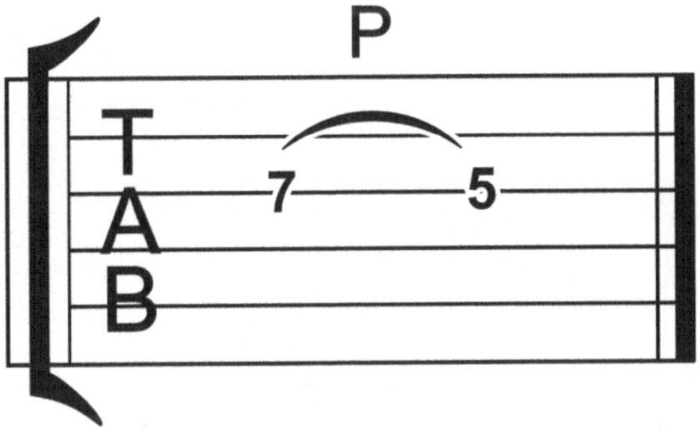

This is the same as the hammer-on example, but in reverse. Start by placing your first finger on the fifth fret of the third string (G) **and** your third finger on the seventh fret of the same string. You should now have two fingers on the G string.

Play the note on the seventh fret with your pick. Then, as you lift your finger, pluck the string slightly with the fingertip of your third finger so that you clearly hear the note on the fifth fret.

As with hammer-ons, the letter 'P' is not always included; sometimes it is only a curved line. If no letters are shown, the numbers will indicate if it is a hammer-on or pull-off. If the first note is lower than the second, it is a hammer-on; if it is higher, it is a pull-off.

The Sketchy Version

```
e|------------|
B|------------|
G|----7p5----|
D|------------|
A|------------|
E|------------|
```

Wait. I know what you're thinking: can you play both of them together? Well, of course you can, but the answer isn't just yeah, it's "Oh Yeah!" Magic happens when you mix these two techniques in a solo.

When combined, they look like this in TAB notation. Remember, you only need to pluck the first note with the pick. This gives you three notes from one pick of a string!

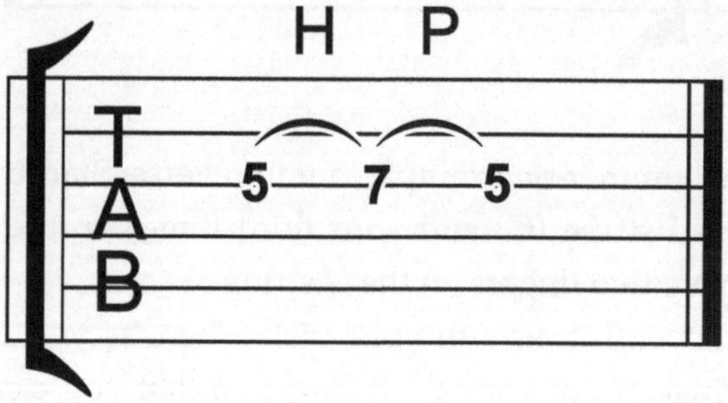

The Sketchy Version

```
e|------------|
B|------------|
G|--5h7p5----|
D|------------|
A|------------|
E|------------|
```

SLIDES (/ OR \)

Slides or shift slides, as they are also known, are one of my favorite techniques. That's why I'm going to give you a little tip I wish I'd known when I was starting out. But first things first, what's a slide? Well, it's a technique in which you pick a note and then slide a finger of your fretting hand to another note on the same string before picking it.

This is usually done with notes that are quite close together on the neck, but some guitarists, such as John Mayer, slide a full octave or more in some of his explosive guitar medleys. I'm not suggesting that you slide like that, let's take it easy until you get to kill it live like he does.

So, here's the great tip I promised you for slides: learn some common pentatonic patterns horizontally. That way, you can use slides to move through a scale, going up or down the neck.

I was backstage at a festival when I heard a guy from another band saying, "I'm playing the same notes, but horizontally!" Thinking about scales in that way unlocked a whole new playing universe for me.

Here's what it looks like:

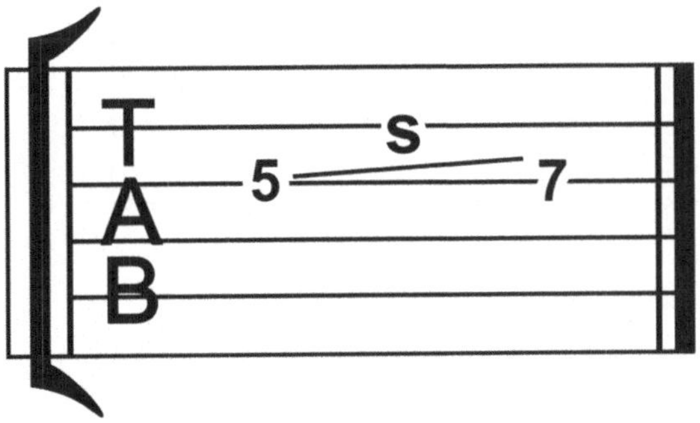

The Sketchy Version

```
e|------------|
B|------------|
G|--5/7-------|
D|------------|
A|------------|
E|------------|
```

You can slide up... ...or down

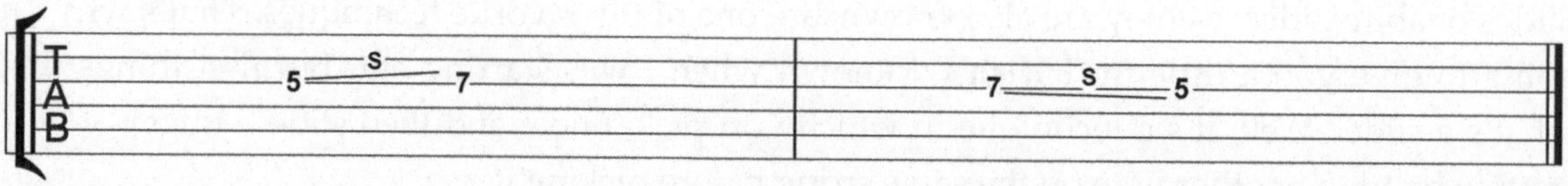

Slides are sometimes written in TAB as only a slanted line or with the letters 'sl.' instead of 's' above the line.

The Sketchy Version

```
e|------------|
B|------------|
G|--5/7 - 7/5--|
D|------------|
A|------------|
E|------------|
```

LEGATO SLIDE

This is distinguished from the shift slide because the second note is created purely by the action of the slide, and is not picked. This results in two notes from a single pick of the string.

Legato slides produce a smoother sound than a shift slide and are shown in TAB as:

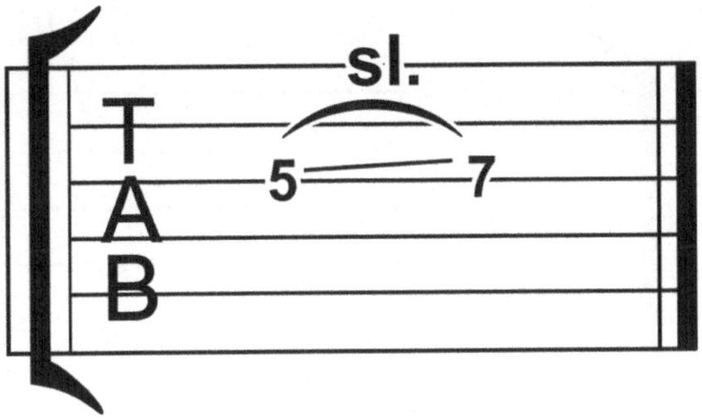

Legato slides can also be shown with the letter 's' over the curved line, or without any letters.

BENDS (B)

Ladies and gentlemen, please take a bow as the most emotional guitar move of all time enters the room. It doesn't matter if you love crazy bends, such as Gary Moore or Stevie Ray, or prefer more delicate ones like David Gilmour; what's important is bending at just the right moment and making sure it sounds great.

How do you bend a string? Well, you simply play a note and then move a finger up or down, bending the string from its original position, and raising the note in pitch. Speaking of which, you can bend a half tone, a full tone, a tone and a half, or even two entire tones.

Don't worry, TAB wizards like us know how much to bend a note, because it's indicated on the TAB:

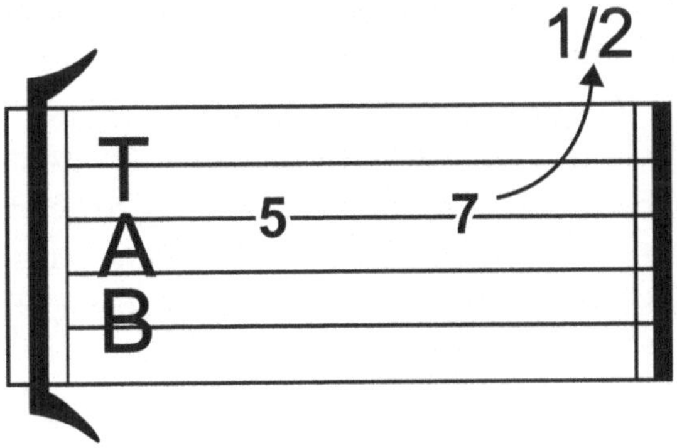

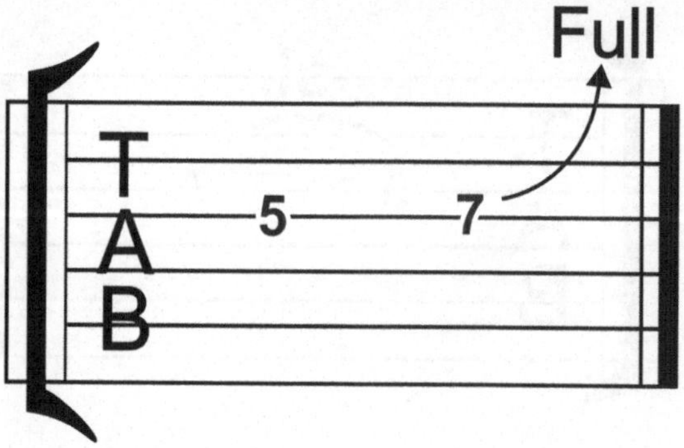

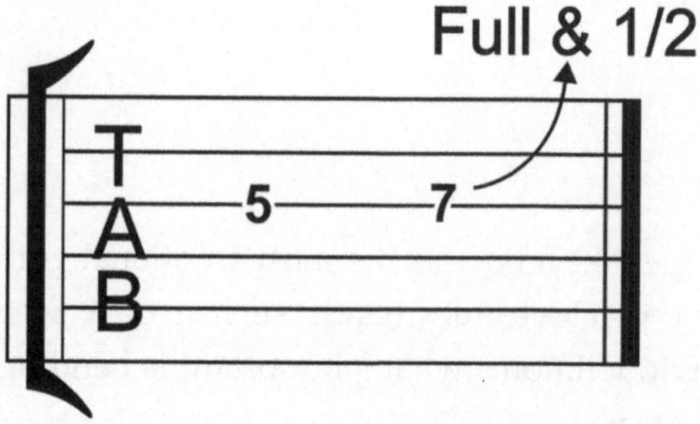

There are also some other bends that you might see in TABs, such as the number '2' to represent a two-tone bend, or a '1/4' bend, which is only a very slight bend of the string.

If you're not sure how a full tone bend differs from a tone and a half bend, it's all about the note you hear after the bend is complete. For example, a half tone bend on a C note would produce a C#, a full tone would result in a D, a tone and a half would give you a D#, and a finger strength testing two-tone bend ends up with a D#.

To practice bending in tune, play the target note first, for example, for a half-tone bend, play the note that is one fret up from the note you're going to bend, and remember the pitch. Now, go back a fret and bend the note until you hear the same pitch. Do the same by going up two frets for the full tone bend, three for the tone-and-a-half bend, etc.

Pro Tip: If you're playing one of the more extreme bends, such as a tone and a half or two tones, use two fingers, not one, to bend the note. It will give you more strength, and most importantly, a lot more control to get the bend perfectly in tune.

Believe me, bending is a one-way ride; there's no turning back. In my case, as soon as I learned the technique, it became my thing. Imagine being able to make your guitar speak; well, bends are the tonal inflections that set the mood, send the message, and allow your guitar to talk!

The Sketchy Version

When it's not specified, then it's a full-tone bend.

```
e|------------|
B|------------|
G|--5b7------|
D|------------|
A|------------|
E|------------|
```

When you see something like "1/2" after the (b), that means half a tone. Easy, right?

```
e|------------|
B|------------|
G|--5b1/2-7---|
D|------------|
A|------------|
E|------------|
```

BEND AND RELEASE (BR)

This is an extension to the bends we just covered, but after completing the bend, you keep pressure on the note while slowly releasing it, returning it to its original position and pitch.

It takes a while to master, but it's well worth the effort, because it's superb for highly emotional playing and needs to be in every guitarist's bag of tricks. Here it is in TAB:

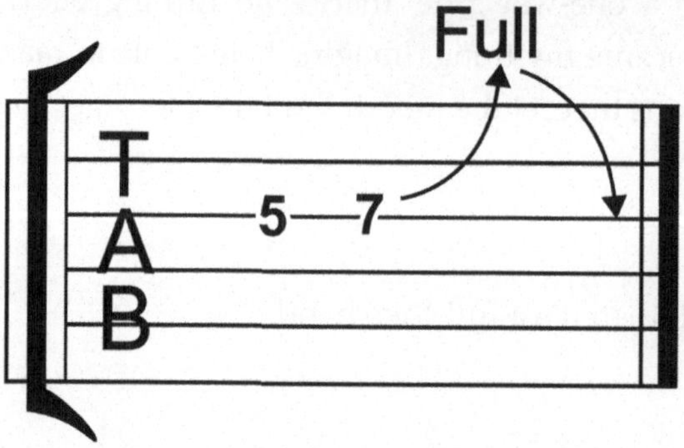

In some TABs, the letter 'r' is also sometimes included above or next to the curved release line.

The Sketchy Version

```
e|-------------|
B|-------------|
G|--5--7b(9)r--|
D|-------------|
A|-------------|
E|-------------|
```

PRE-BEND (PB)

This is another variation, but this time, you bend the string before it is played. For example, bend the 7th fret of the G string up a whole tone; this is the pre-bend, then play the bent note. This is then usually released in the same way as the bend and release we just looked at. Here's what it looks like in TAB:

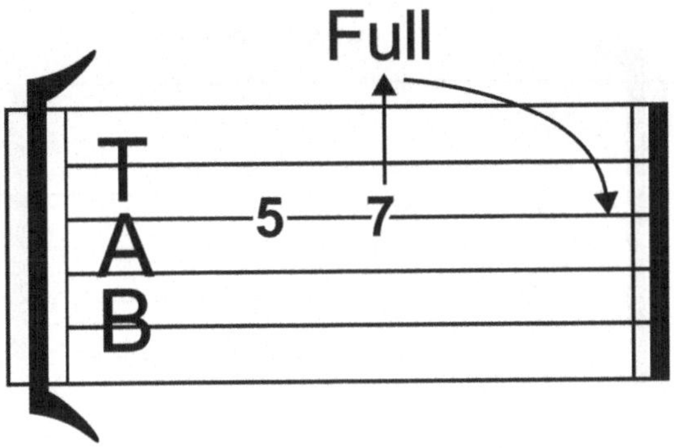

The letters 'pb' are sometimes also included in the TAB to indicate a pre bend.

The Sketchy Version

```
e|-------------|
B|-------------|
G|--5--7pb9r7-|
D|-------------|
A|-------------|
E|-------------|
```

VIBRATO

Vibrato can be created in a few different ways, either by shaking one of your finger tips horizontally. Or, if a wider vibrato is required (or you prefer the technique), by ever so slightly bending and releasing the string numerous times. You can also create vibrato using the whammy bar, if you have one, but we'll get to that soon.

This is how vibrato is shown in TAB:

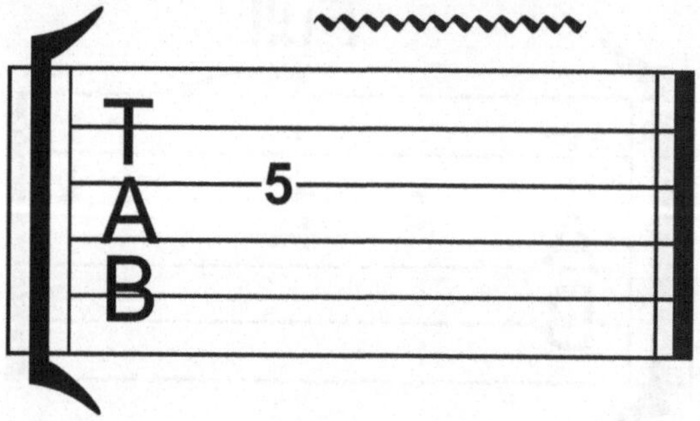

Or, if it's a wide vibrato, it will look like this:

The word 'vib' is also sometimes added above either of the wavy lines to indicate vibrato.

The Sketchy Version

```
e| ------------|
B| ------------|
G| --5~~~~~~~~--|
D| ------------|
A| ------------|
E| ------------|
```

GHOST NOTE

Ghost notes are percussive sounds that have no distinct pitch. They are usually created by lightly touching a string with the fretting hand without fully pressing down on a fret, producing a muted scratch or click instead of a distinct musical note.

In TAB, they are usually indicated as:

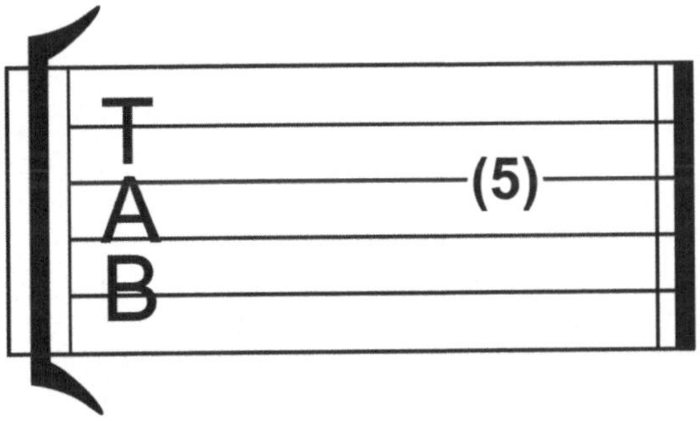

The Sketchy Version

```
e|-------------|
B|-------------|
G|------(5)---|
D|-------------|
A|-------------|
E|-------------|
```

DEAD NOTE

Much like ghost notes, dead notes are also muted, percussive sounds with no distinct pitch. They are also created by lightly touching or dampening a string with your fretting hand, stopping the note from vibrating freely. However, unlike a ghost note, the dead note is then picked, which can make it louder in volume than a ghost note.

In TAB, they are indicated as:

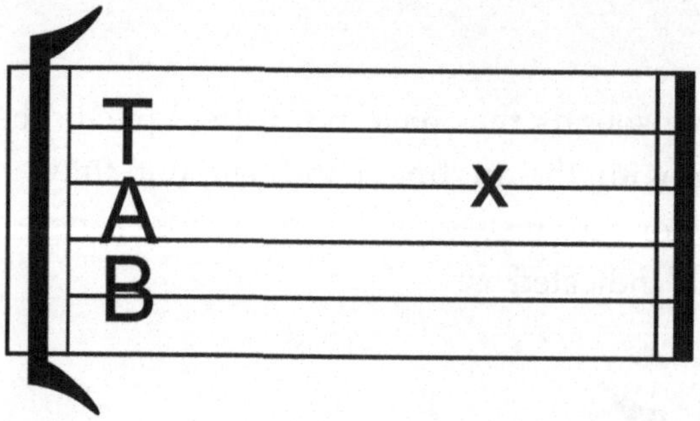

The Sketchy Version

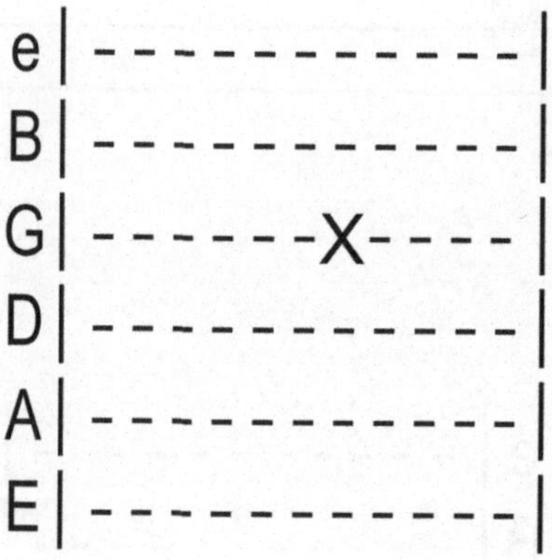

PALM MUTE

Palm muting involves gently laying the side of the palm of your strumming hand over the strings, on or near the bridge, so that they are slightly muted. When picked or strummed, it creates a super-cool 'chugg' sound.

This is what it looks like in TAB:

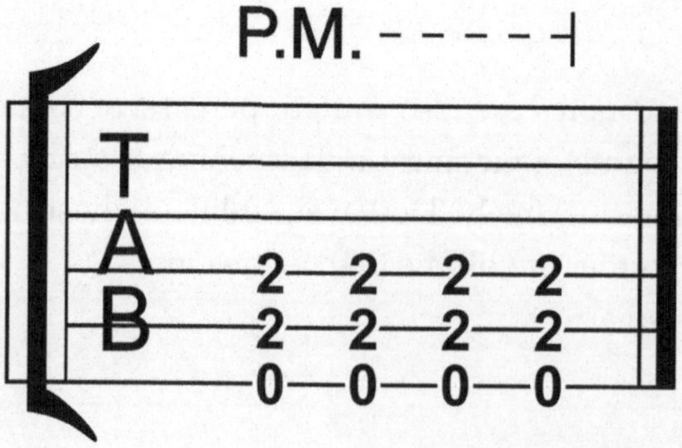

If only a single note needs to be palm muted, there will be P.M. (or PM) above it, and there will be no dashed line afterwards.

The Sketchy Version

```
   Palm Mute-------------|
e|-------------|
B|-------------|
G|-------------|
D|-2--2--2--2-|
A|-2--2--2--2-|
E|-0--0--0--0-|
```

LET RING

As you've probably guessed, Let Ring indicates that you should allow a certain note (or notes) to carry on vibrating until it fades out naturally. It's shown in TAB as:

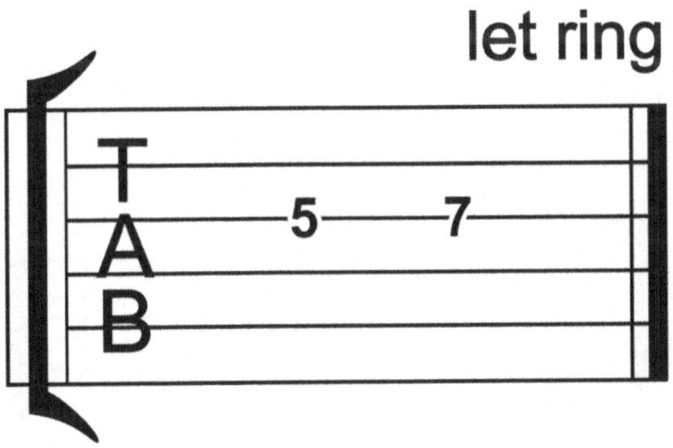

Let Ring is also sometimes abbreviated to 'l.v.'.

HARMONICS

You can create two different types of harmonics on a guitar: natural and pinched. Natural harmonics involve placing the fleshy part of a finger of your fretting hand above certain positions on the neck, such as directly above the 12th fret, then very gently touching a string with that finger as you pick it. In TAB, it looks like this:

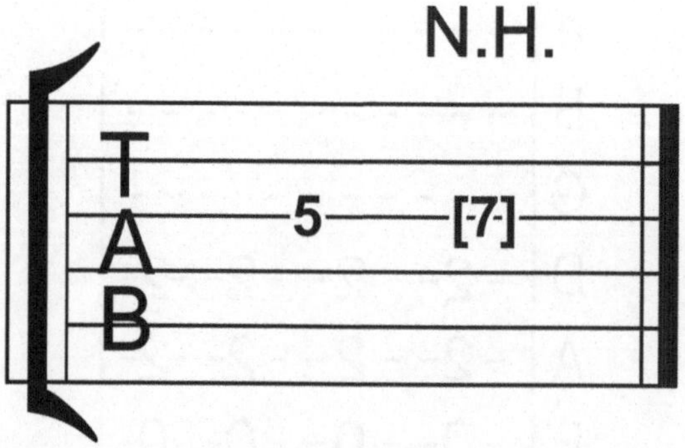

Sometimes, a natural harmonic is shown in square brackets without 'N.H.' above it, or even without the square brackets and only the 'N.H.' Round brackets - '(7)' - are also used in some TAB software, and the word 'Harm.' above the note occasionally replaces the 'N.H.'.

Pinch harmonics involve picking a note, then allowing the fleshy part of the side of the thumb of your picking hand to make contact with the string immediately afterward to create the harmonic.

They are often called squeals because of the sound they make. Check out any song featuring either Zakk Wylde or Dimebag Darrell, who were both masters of pinched harmonics. Here they are in TAB:

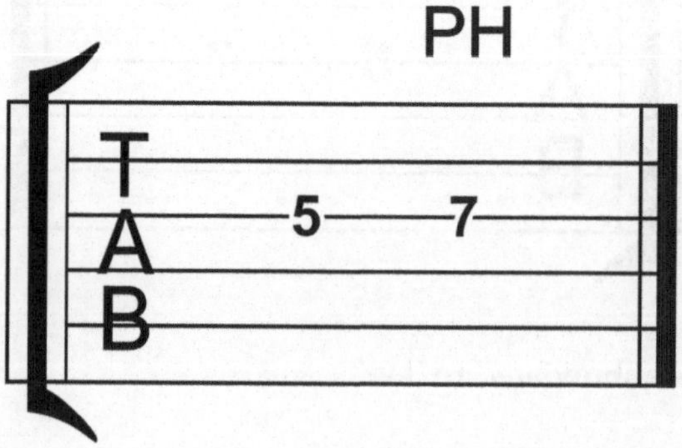

Pinch harmonics can also be shown by placing the note in a diamond, or by using 'ph' instead of 'PH' above the pinched note.

The Sketchy Version

```
e|------------|
B|------------|
G|--5--<7>---|
D|------------|
A|------------|
E|------------|
```

DOWNSTROKE AND UPSTROKE

These are downward or upward picks of a string and are shown in TAB as a halved square for downstrokes and a 'V' for upstrokes:

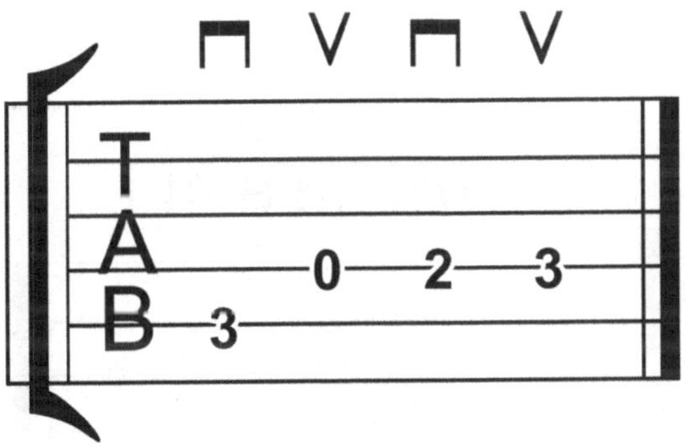

Some TAB software shows downstrokes and upstrokes as arrows.

TAPPING

This involves using a finger (or fingers) from your strumming/picking hand to tap a note on the fretboard. Most players usually use their index finger to do this, holding their pick between their thumb and middle finger. It's the same motion as tapping on the screen of your smartphone, but your target is a particular fret and string. Here it is in TAB:

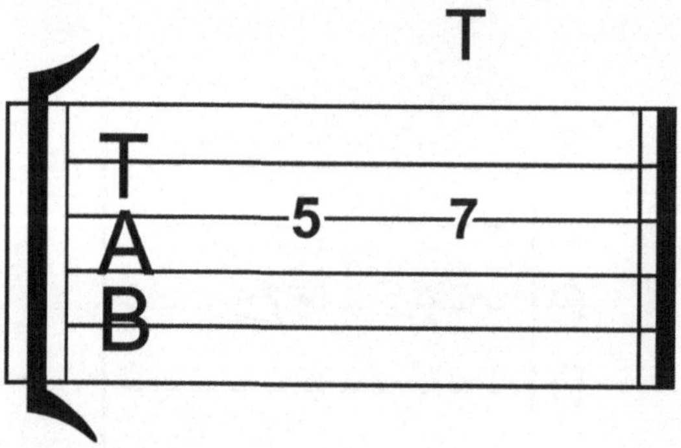

Depending on what software was used to create the TAB, the 'T' may be placed in a circle. And some TABs may show tapping with a '+' symbol, but this is uncommon.

FINGERING

Picking and fretting hand fingering is sometimes indicated in TAB, especially if the song involves complex patterns.

Picking hand fingering is shown with the letters - *p i m a* - representing the thumb (pulgar in Spanish), index (indice), middle (medio), and ring (anular). Rarely, *c* will also be included, representing the pinkie (chiquito).

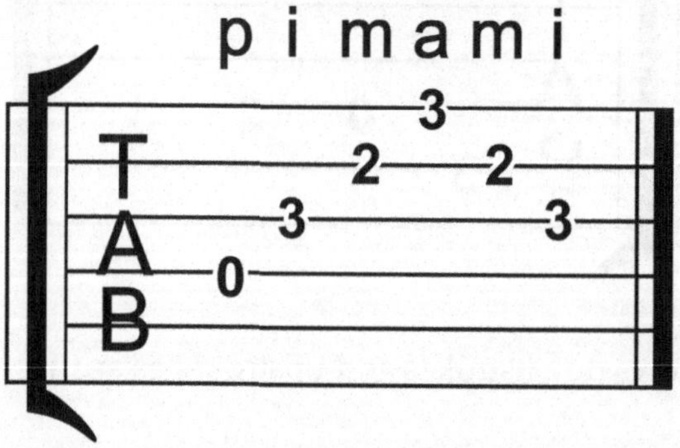

Fretting hand fingering is shown with numbers - 1 to 4 - and 'T' for the thumb.

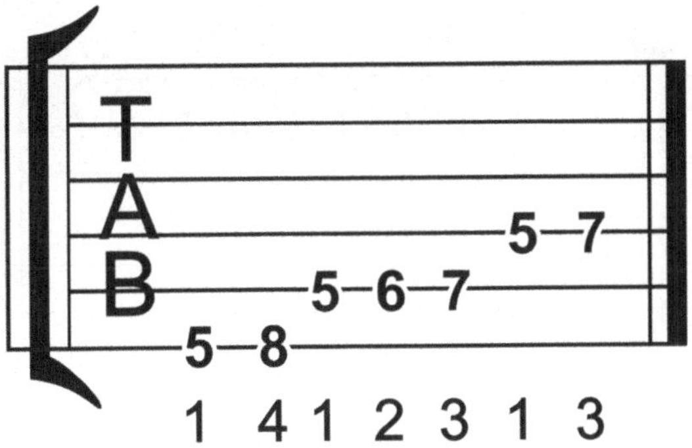

PICK SCRAPE

Pick scrapes involve, as you've probably guessed, scraping your pick along the length of the strings, either up or down the neck.

They are usually played on the low E, A, and D strings, creating a scraping sound as the pick moves across the thicker strings. They understandably don't sound too hot if you try playing them on the thinner, smoother strings. In TAB, they are indicated as:

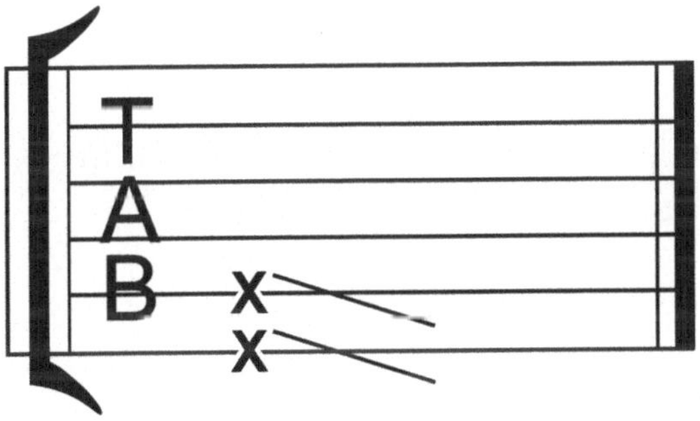

In some tabs, a wiggly line is used instead of a straight one. They can also be shown by placing the letters 'PS' above the 'X' symbol.

TRILL

Trills are a rapid succession of hammer-ons and pull-offs, usually played using two notes on the same string. They can be indicated as either:

Or:

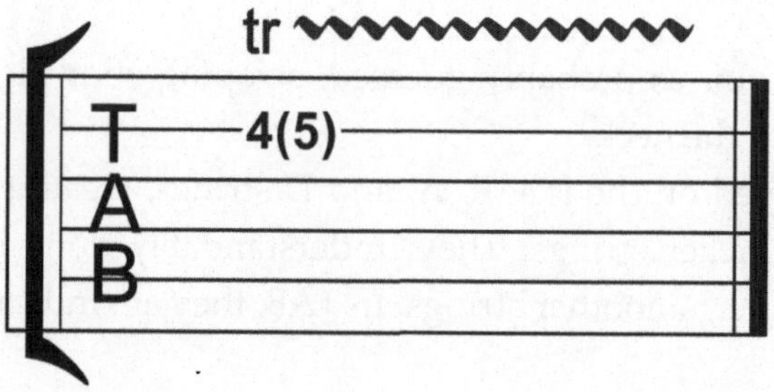

TREMOLO BAR DIP

If your guitar is fitted with a tremolo system, you can use it to create everything from subtle vibrato to full-on dive bombs. In TAB, it's usually indicated as:

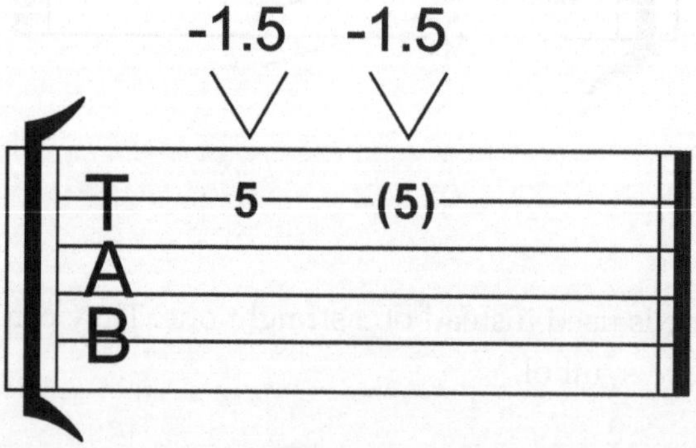

The words 'w/bar' or 'dive w/bar' might also be placed above the notes along with the symbols or alone.

A larger 'V' is also sometimes used, showing the start note, the amount of pitch change, and the end note:

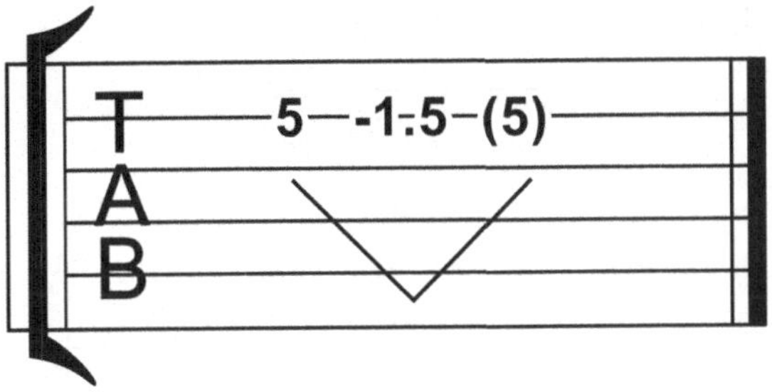

The direction is shown by either a plus or a minus number above the 'V'. Pull back, raising the pitch, for a positive number; dive, lowering the pitch, for a negative number. As with bends, the amount of pitch change is indicated in tones, from 1/2 a tone (one fret), to a full tone (two frets), to as many tones as you want to pull or dive!

To download a printable version of our cheatsheet with all the symbols go to **playfirstnote.com/bonuses.**

HOW TO PLAY THE RHYTHM PART IN TABS?

TABs are fantastic, but there are a few things that let them down, the main one being the lack of specific information on the placement and length of each note or chord.

Every note in standard music notation has a specific value; for example, it might be played for the duration of 4 beats, 2 beats, a single beat, or even half a beat, an eighth of a beat, or whatever. TAB, being a more basic way of writing music, doesn't include this.

So how do I know when or for how long to play a note or chord using TAB?

Even though it isn't precise, most quality TABs have the notes laid out in a way that suggests how they should be played.

If, for example, there are 8 notes in a bar of TAB and they are all the same distance from each other, they will probably all be played for the same duration. Whereas, if the bar has one note at the beginning and another two at the very end of a bar, the first one will usually need to be played and held for a lot longer than the final two.

In most cases, you are probably looking at a TAB because you want to learn a particular riff, song, or solo. This is where the magic of TAB comes into its own; you don't need to read the duration value of each note, you just listen to the song, and you'll know how long each note should be played for.

The TAB tells you what note or chord you need to play; you pick the timing and rhythm up from listening to the song you want to learn.

But, sometimes basic rhythm information is included in Tablature, for example, take a look at this chord sequence:

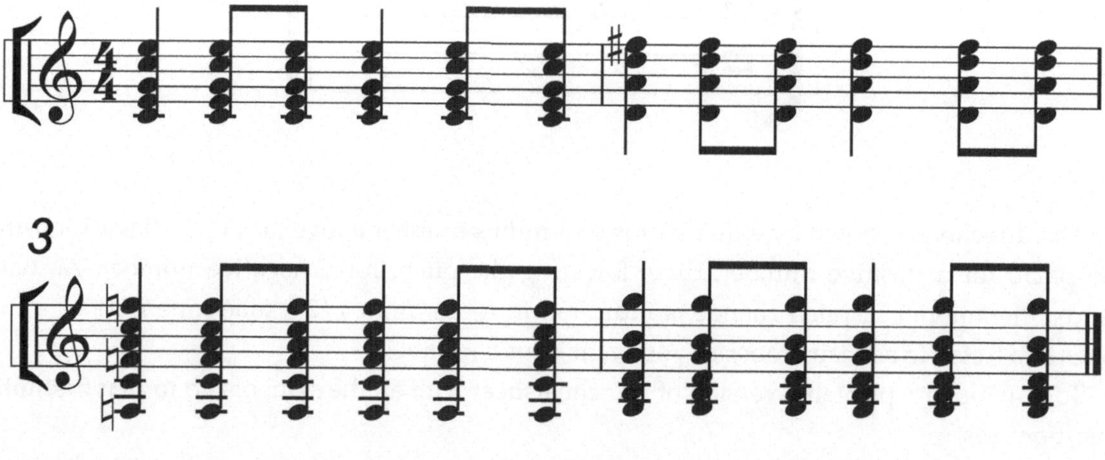

It looks like rocket science, doesn't it? Well, let's translate it into a language we now know well, TAB notation. I'm just going to add the strumming pattern above the chords.

To download the audio file for the following notation, head to **playfirstnote.com/bonuses.**

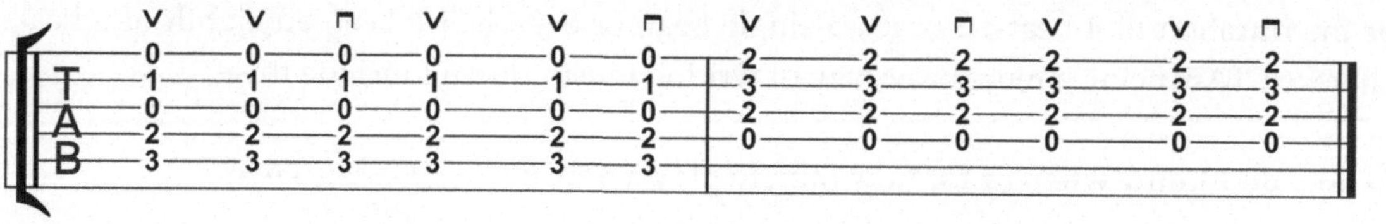

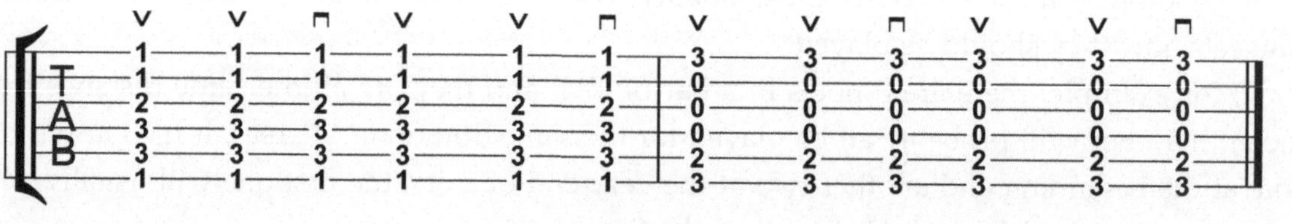

Even though TAB is far more basic than notation, it's a superb roadmap to use along with listening to a song you want to learn on YouTube, Spotify, or wherever. The TAB gives you the info on what to play, and the song is your timing guide and metronome - it's all you need to start playing and stop dreaming.

CHAPTER 3
HOW TO READ AND PLAY TABS

FROM SIMPLE MELODIES TO POWERFUL CHORDS, ONE STEP AT A TIME

OK, this is it; it's showtime.

You might be feeling exactly like I did back in the day, the first time I stepped on stage in front of screaming fans: Knees shaky, palms sweaty. But worry not, because I'm here for you. I've walked this path many, many times before, and I'm going to give you all the tips and tricks I wish I'd been given back then, so you won't encounter the same pitfalls I did.

What comes next? Well, just me doing my best to pour decades of playing experience with TABs into simple exercises you'll master in a day.

Ready or not, here we go!

SIMPLE MELODIES

There's endless fun to be had once you get to work with TABs, but it all starts here, with a simple melody. Don't worry, you should be able to play it effortlessly. I'm sure you're familiar with "Mary Had a Little Lamb". It's one of those nursery rhymes that's just part of our DNA.

Let's use this simple, timeless piece of music to work on your TAB reading skills.

We'll only be using the second string (B), so you can focus on your left hand moving up and down the fretboard following what's indicated in the TAB. It might look complex, but when you get your head around it, which doesn't take too long, it's a piece of cake; *you got this*!

To download the melodies mentioned in this section, head to **playfirstnote.com/bonuses.**

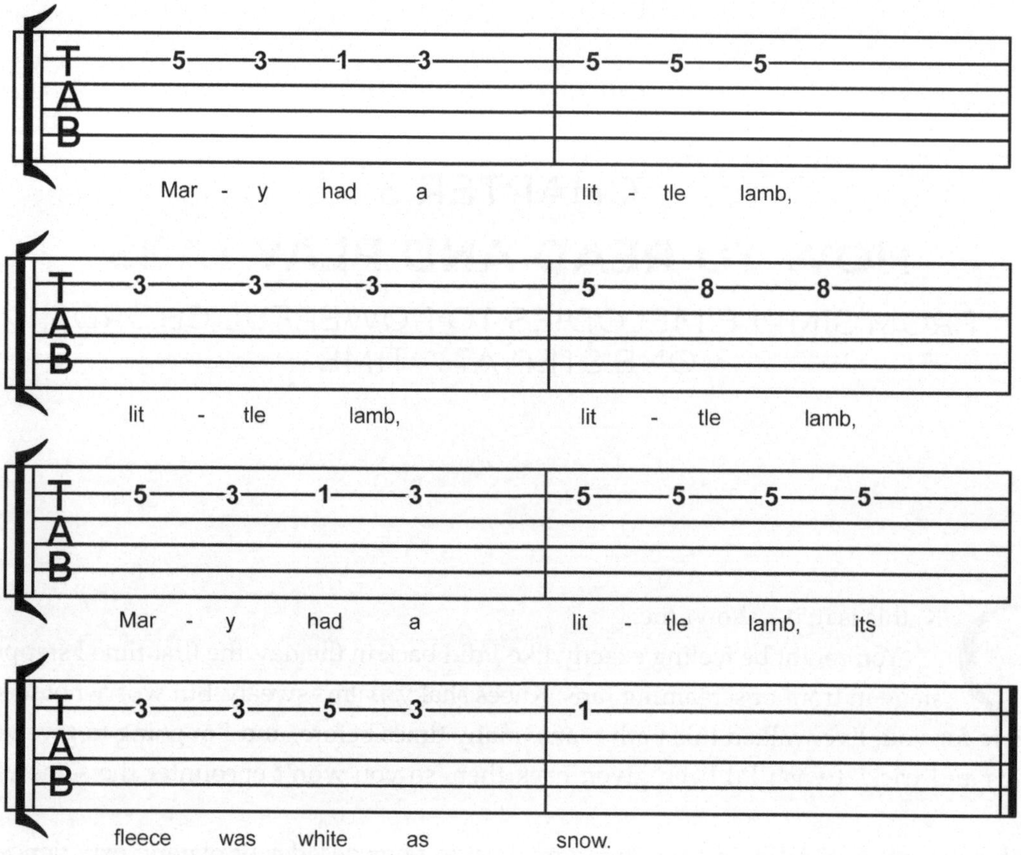

Hey, we're here to practice, right? So, here's another classic as a one-string exercise. This one is "Row, Row, Row Your Boat". I'm sure you know it by heart, but here's a little guide on how to play it using only the (high) e string.

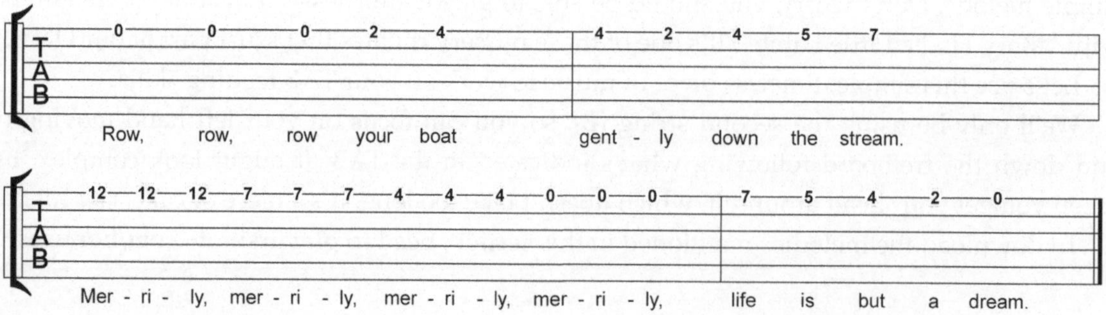

Let's elevate the fun factor by blending in some of the stuff you learned earlier. It's like adding a pinch of spice to these timeless classics. So, what are we using? Well, since we're staying in one string, why don't we use some slide techniques?

This is the same TAB but with the slide move between some of the notes. It not only *looks* different, but it also *sounds* different, right?

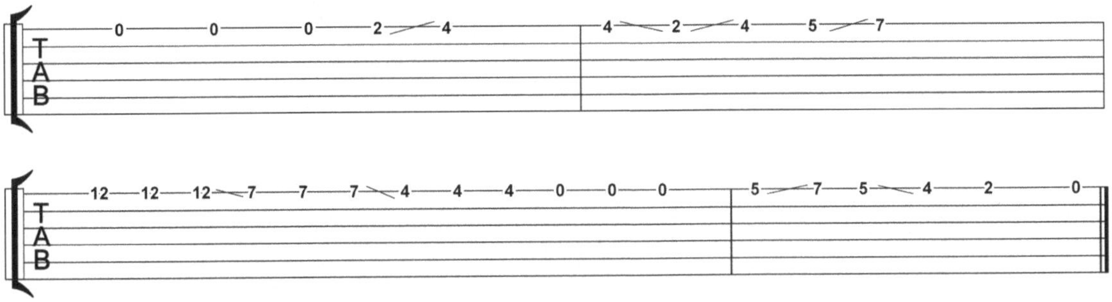

OK, now that you've mastered those two melodies, it's time to raise the bar. Don't worry, we're not stepping in Joe Satriani's shoes just yet (those mirror-like glasses will have to wait just a little bit longer, mate).

You'll be playing "Baa Baa Black Sheep" using the top three strings of your guitar.

Yes, you'll have to change strings a bit and mind the picking hand, but, hey, you'll be a whole step closer to being a guitar hero (remember that Joe started this way, too!).

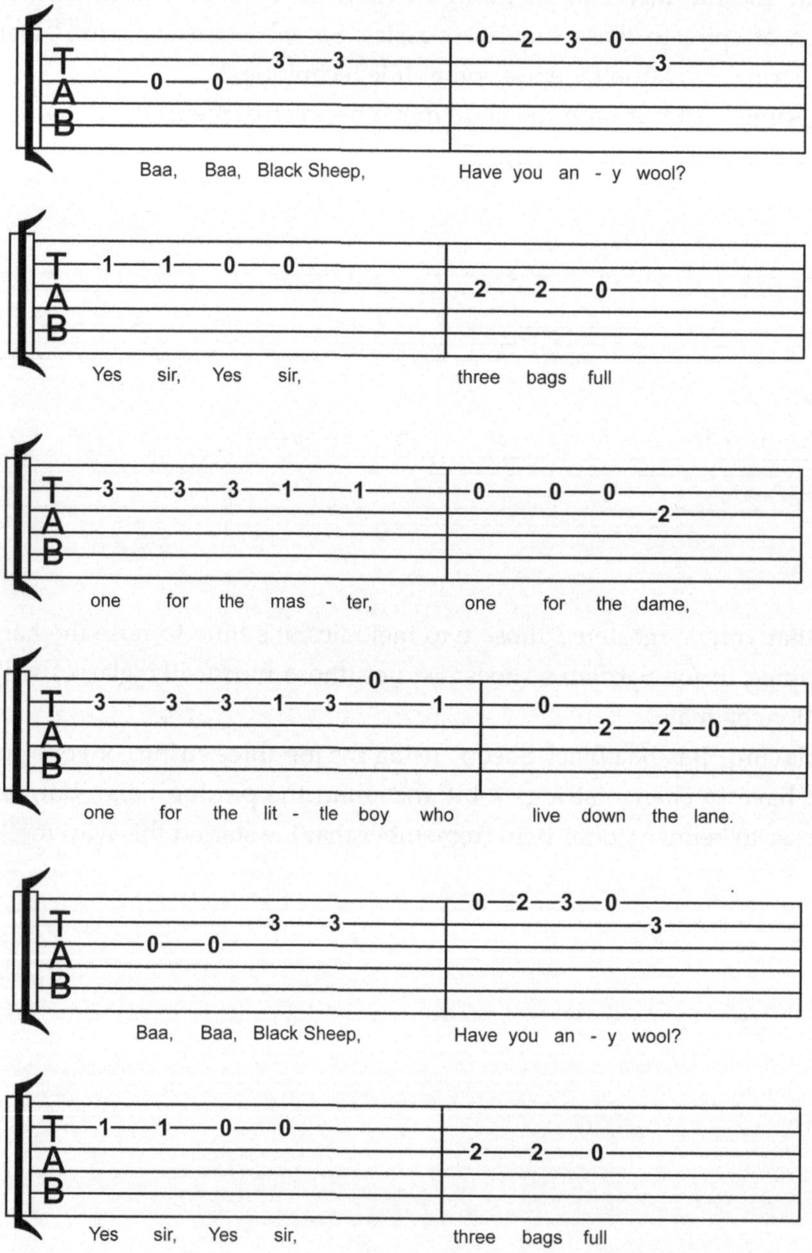

CHORDS, CHORDS, AND MORE CHORDS!

I know what you're thinking, "We've covered chords already!" Well, that was the sneak peek, the preview, the trailer, if you like!

Chords are a full-blown multi-episode series ready to receive every Emmy Award ever.

I've shown you some easy open chords and a few barre chords. Coming up next, we have some very useful, great-sounding chords, how they're written in TAB notation, and how to spot them on the fly.

So, let's work on them for a bit and have some fun strumming that good-old six-stringer of yours.

Suspended Chords

Suspended chords are your new best friends. Believe me, once you discover their magic, it's difficult to stop using them everywhere. They're usually called "sus" chords, and I'm sure you've heard them in many songs.

For example, the intro riff of "Crazy Little Thing Called Love" by Queen is made of a D followed by a Dsus4.

What does Dsus4 stand for? I'm glad you asked. Let's go through some very basic chord theory to explain it.

The D major chord contains three notes: D - F# - A. That's the major triad: the root or tonic naming the chord (D), the third note of the major scale (F#), and the fifth note of the major scale (A).

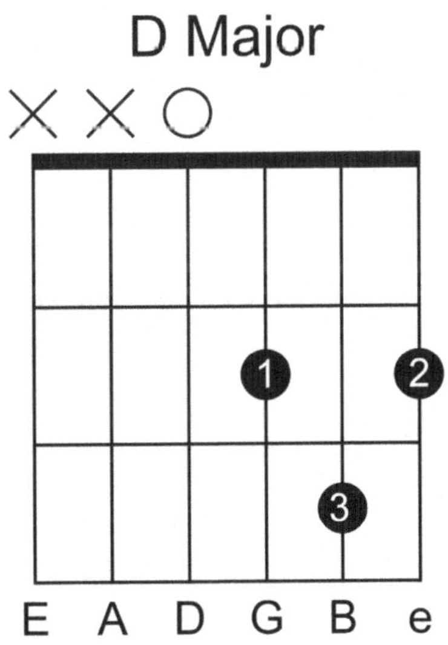

If we want to make it a minor chord, we can flatten the third note of the major scale, changing the F# to an F, right?

D Minor

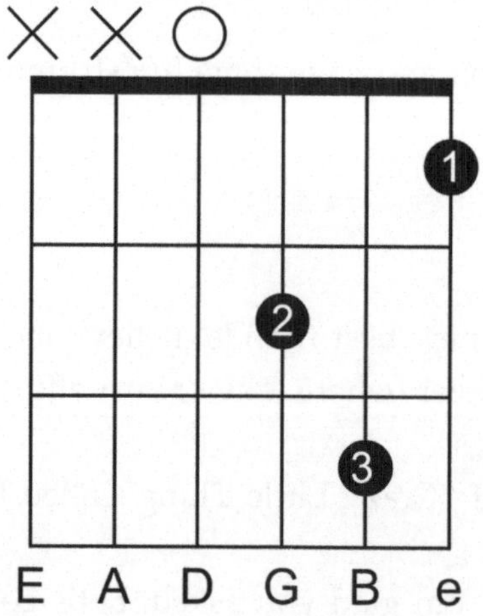

Those two chords sound very different. But what if, instead of using a major or minor (flat) third, you use the second note of the major scale (E) or the fourth note (G)? That's right, you get a chord that's neither major nor minor, but "suspended".

If you use the second (E), it's a sus2 chord, and if you use the fourth (G), that's a sus4.

So, without further ado, here are Dsus2 and Dsus4 in all their suspended glory.

Dsus2

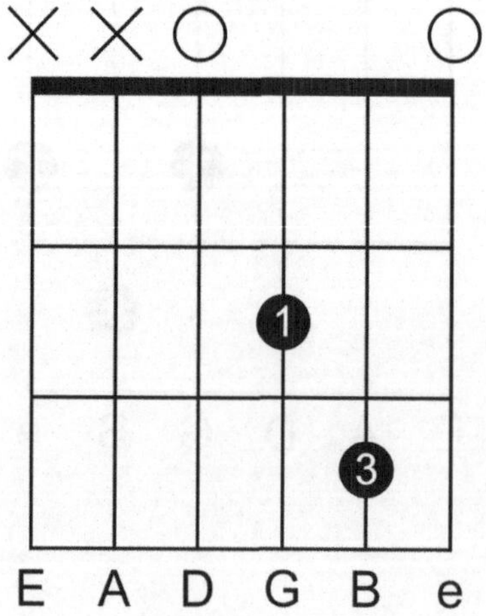

Dsus4

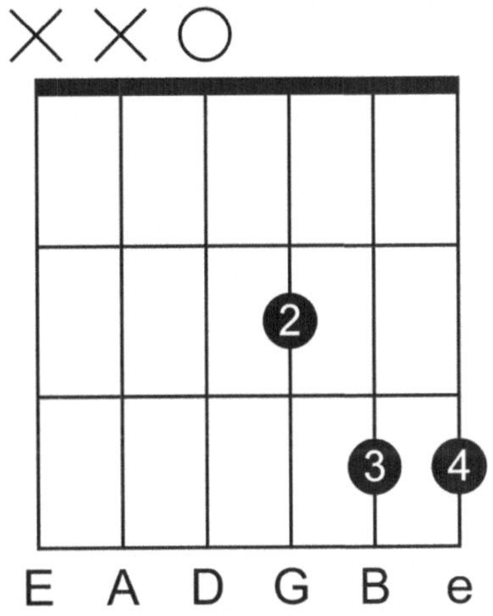

Let's practice them. The following exercise starts with the major, moves to the minor, then to the sus2, and finally, the sus4, all within 4 bars.

To download the audio files for exercises in this section, please visit **playfirstnote.com/bonuses.**

Note: If you need more info on reading chord diagrams, check out the Appendix.

Exercise 1

Do you notice anything unusual? Well, the picking pattern is an arpeggio, which is a broken chord whose notes need to be picked. Therefore, instead of strumming, you need to pick the note pattern shown in the TAB.

Don't worry, once you get used to it, you'll fly through it!

Note: Many TABs have the chord name written above the notes, but I haven't included them because I want you to read every note to familiarize yourself with how TABs work.

Exercise 2

I'm using the same chords for this exercise, but a different pattern. This time, the numbers all form straight lines, indicating that all the strings should be played at the same time.

Therefore, these should be played as chords, so strum them proudly with a big smile on your face!

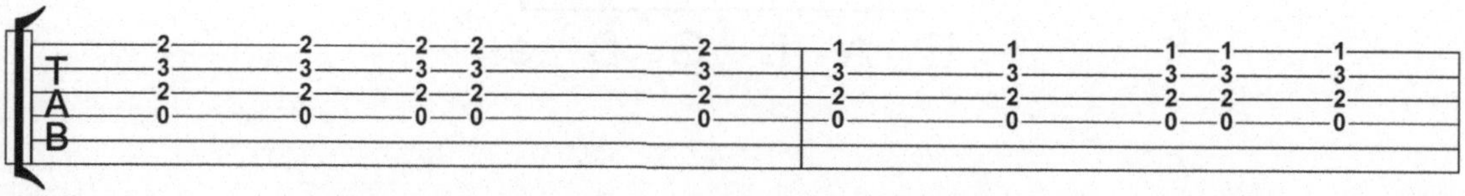

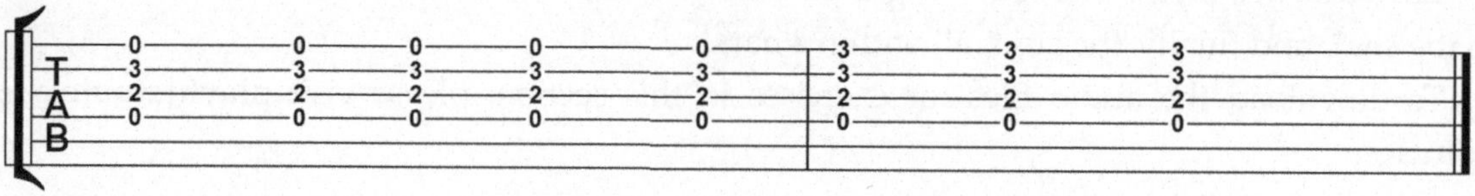

Seventh Chords

The chords I showed you so far are 3-note chords, which we call triads.

But that's not the full story. Some chords need more than three notes to work their magic. Seventh chords are a fantastic example of commonly used, great-sounding 4-note chords that, when used in the right place, create tension within any song.

I know, it all sounds cool, but how do you spot seventh chords in TAB notation?

Let's take it one step at a time. First, we'll learn how to construct a seventh chord, then how to use it, and then how to spot it.

We'll use our trusty old D chord? Alright!

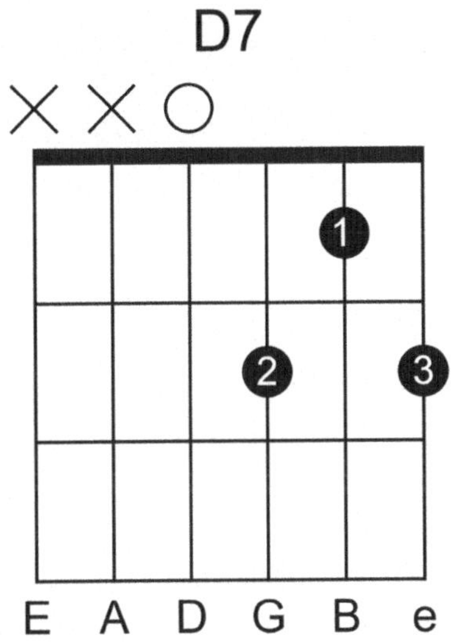

This is a D7 chord. Did you notice that instead of using the D note on the third fret of the second string, as you would for a D major chord, you use the note before the tonic, in this case, the C on the first fret? That's the note creating the tension you feel when listening to the chord.

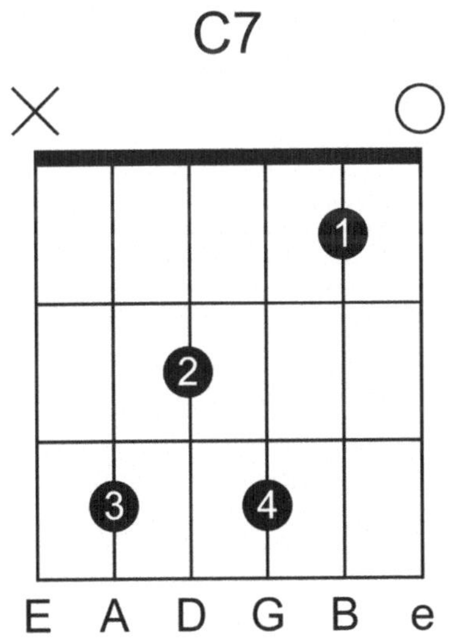

Here's another example, C7. Instead of playing the open third string, you play the Bb, the note before C.

I know what you're thinking, "This is all good, but how do you spot them in TAB notation?" Well, seventh chords can be located by the context, the sound, and the reading.

- **By the context -** They're usually a chord that goes back to the root. Therefore, if you see some odd notes in a chord that's right before the chorus, for example, that's very likely a seventh chord.

- **The sound -** Seventh chords have a unique sound. Try playing a C and then a C7, or a D and then a D7. Do you notice the difference? I know, it's huge! So pay attention to the sense of urgency that seventh chords create.

- **The reading -** Seventh chords on TABs can be recognized by the number of fretted notes. For example, C7 looks very similar to C, but with a slight difference, an extra note. Keep your eyes peeled and you'll spot them right away.

Let's play the major and the seventh version of the good old D in a chord sequence, so you know what it looks and sounds like.

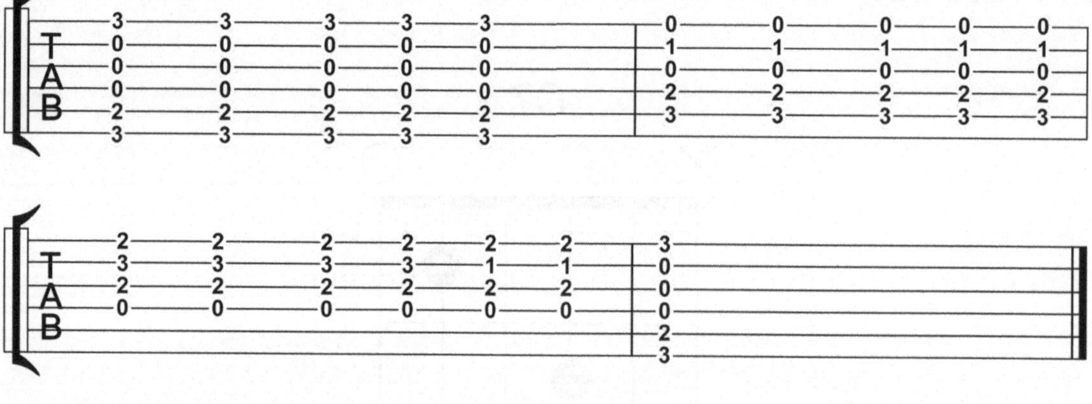

Did you notice the change in the third bar? It starts with a regular D chord, and then changes to D7 before resolving to the big, monumental, beautiful G major chord.

The chord sequence gains momentum and then resolves to the tonic. That's exactly how seventh chords should be used, to take the momentum to the next level and resolve beautifully to the tonic.

Moreover, did you notice, at first glance, that there was something odd about the chords at the end of bar 3? You're making huge progress here! That's what you should be looking for. Seventh chords look like the major version but are ever so slightly different.

In the case of a D major chord in bar 3, the number 1 appearing in the sequence shows you that something has changed, and that change is to the D7 chord.

Barre Chords and Power Chords

Remember our friends, the barre chords? We've already covered them briefly. Well, it's time to go a little deeper.

Do you want to know why? Well, because you'll play barre chords for as long as you play guitar, you'll need to know them inside out.

They've sure rescued me countless times from epic fails. I remember being on stage and absolutely blanking out on the chords of a song, but luckily, the bass player was standing right next to me, so I used barre chords for the rest of the song, simply following the root notes he was playing.

Can you imagine going blank in front of a huge audience? Well, barre chords are your lifeboat in a storm.

But that's not all. I'm going to teach you how to spot and play power chords as well as barre chords. Oh, and stay with me to the end of this chapter because I have a pro tip to share that will make your power chords even more powerful.

Let's get started with barre chords. These can have the root or tonic on the sixth or the fifth string. This is the lowest note within the chord and is played with your index finger; it's also the note that names the chord.

Let's get started with the sixth string before moving to the fifth string.

The coolest thing about barre chords is that once you learn one shape for major, one for minor, and one for seventh chords, you can play any chord you want on the fretboard as long as it has its root on the sixth or fifth string.

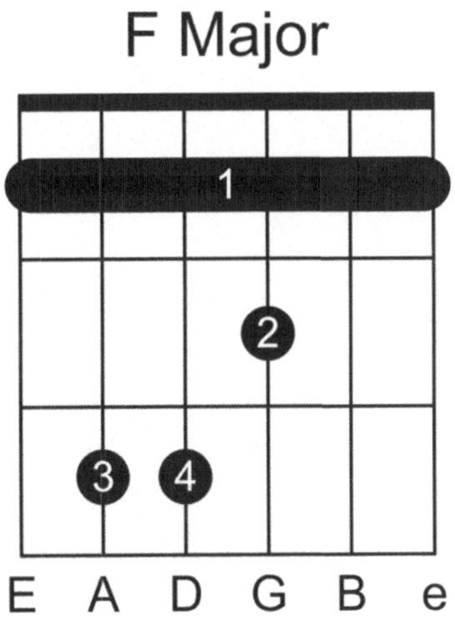

F Minor

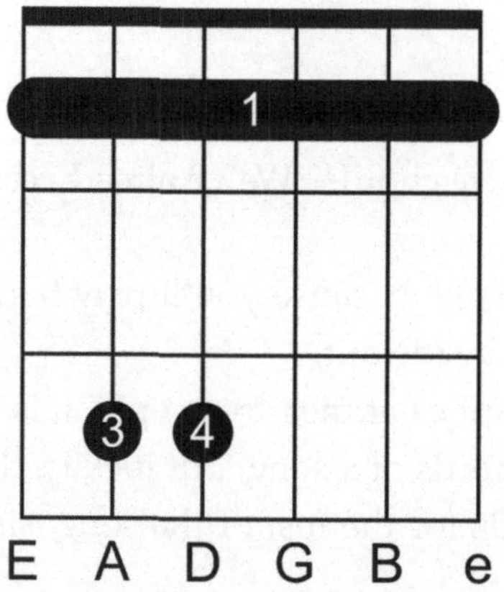

F7

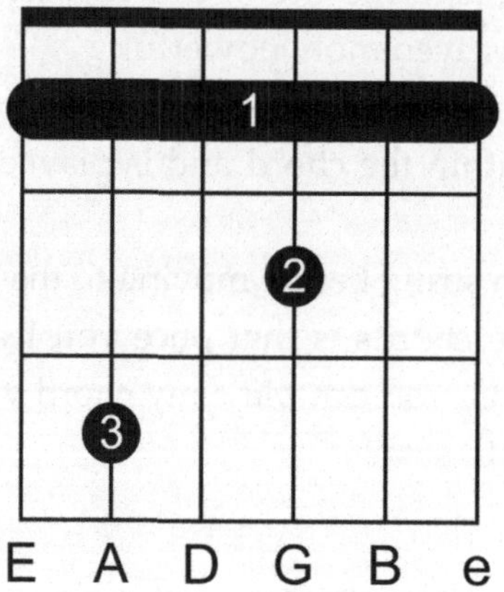

B Major

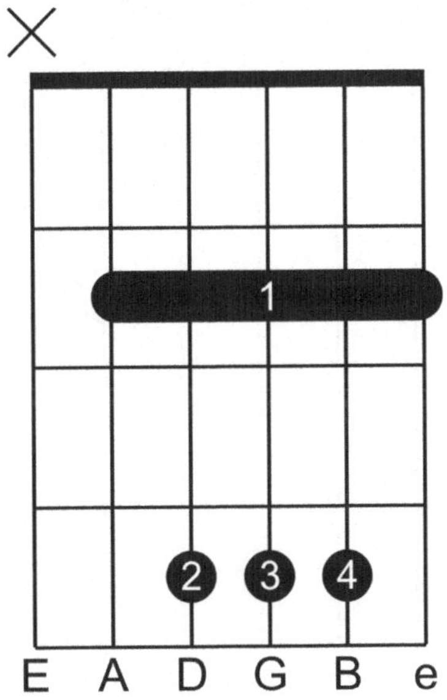

B Minor

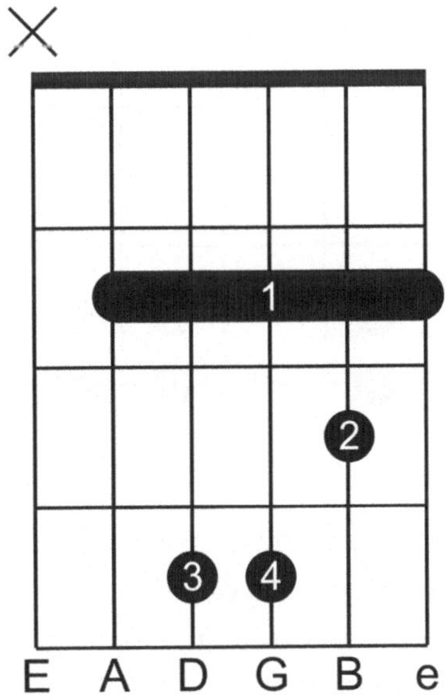

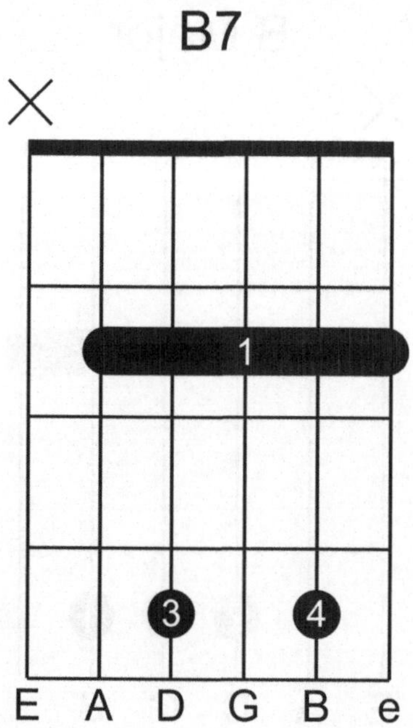

Pro Tip: To play barre chords and power chords, you need to know the names of every note on the sixth and fifth strings. Most players use the fret position markers on their guitar to help them with this; they're super helpful for navigation.

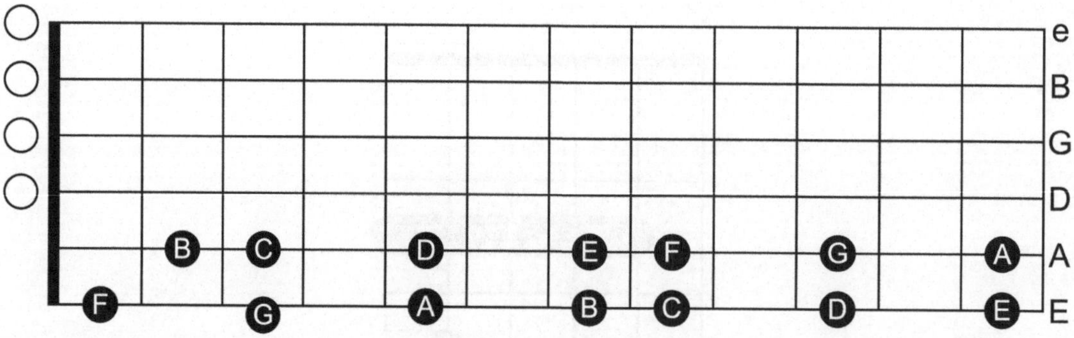

There you go, by memorizing where these notes are, you can instantly play a B minor, an A7, a G major, or any other major, minor, or seventh chord, anywhere on the fretboard.

Moving on to power chords. As you know already, major and minor chords are made of three notes: the root, the third, and the fifth notes of the major scale. Well, the third determines whether the chord is major or minor.

But what if we don't include the third and only play the tonic and the fifth? Well, voilá, you have a power chord. And since they don't contain a third, they're neither minor nor major.

This is what a regular power chord looks like on the sixth and the fifth strings:

F5 (Power Chord)

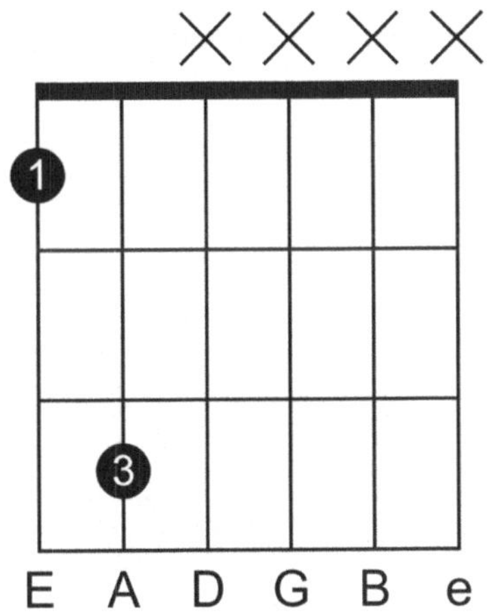

B5 (Power Chord)

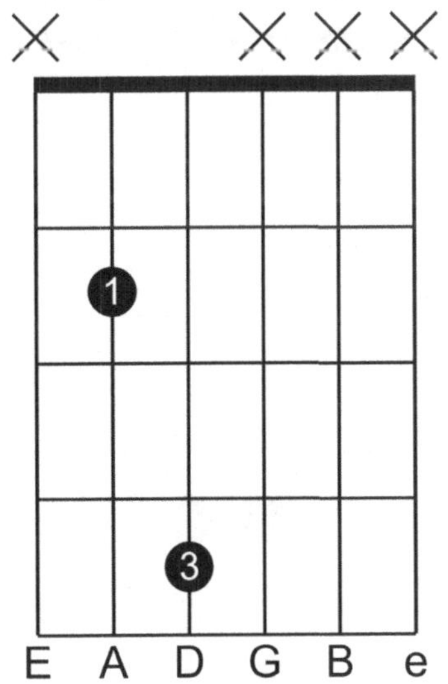

But what if we want even more power from these chords? Well, the note just below the one you're playing with your third finger (the fifth) is the same as the root note. So, if you add that, you'll be playing the same chord with more power. In other words, you're making the chord bigger, fatter, and even more powerful.

F5 (Power Chord)

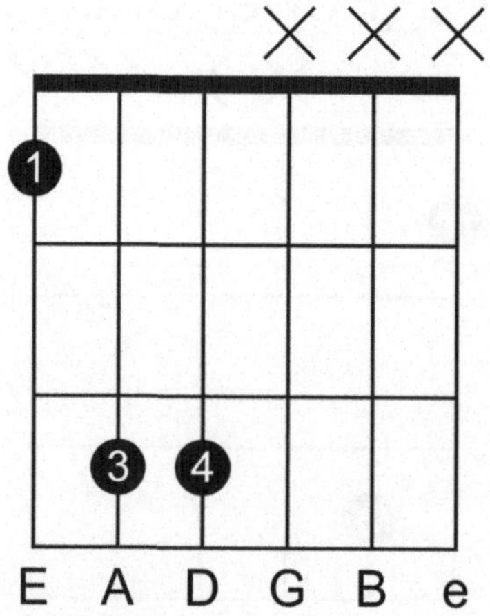

B5 (Power Chord)

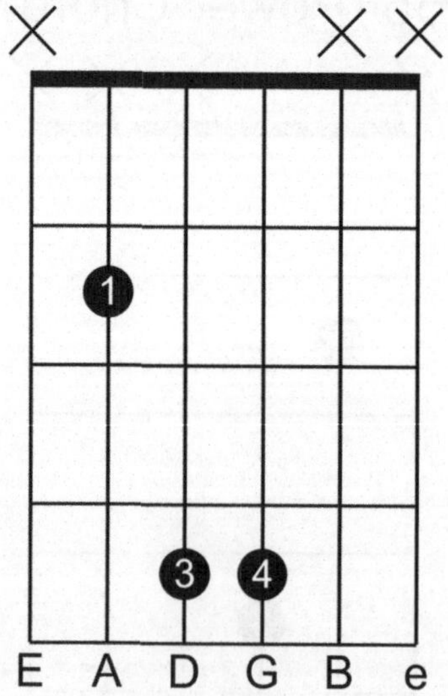

PUTTING CHORDS TO WORK

How can you spot barre and power chords on TABs? Well, the answers to the following questions will give you all the info you need.

- **Are there any zeros in the chord numbers?** If the answer is yes, then you more than likely have an open chord. But keep an eye open for little nuances between them to make sure you're playing exactly the right chords.

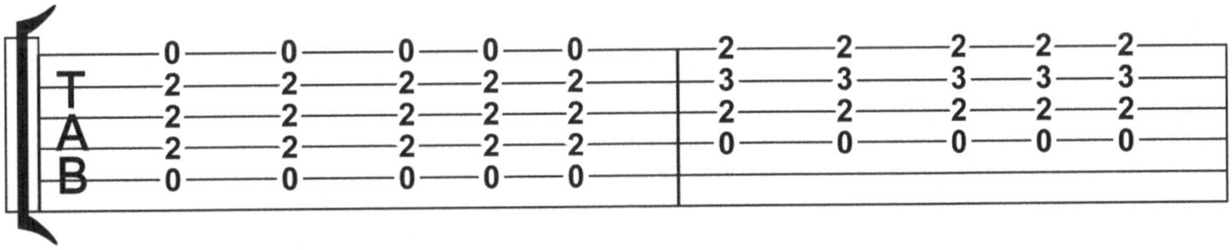

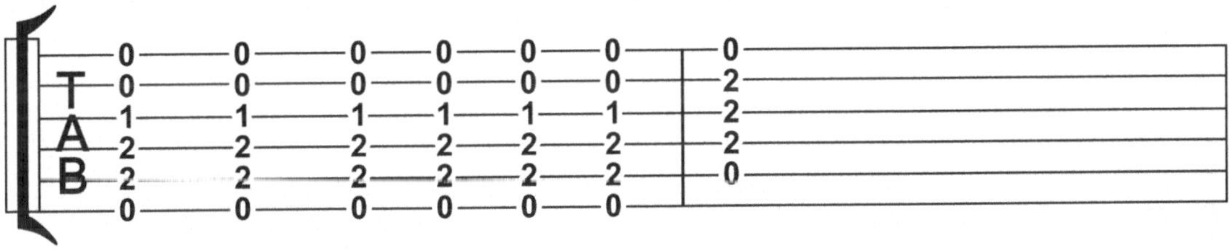

- **Is a number repeating on the top and bottom strings?** If so, you more than likely have a barre chord. Pay attention to the number on the lowest (thickest) string because it will tell you the name of the chord.

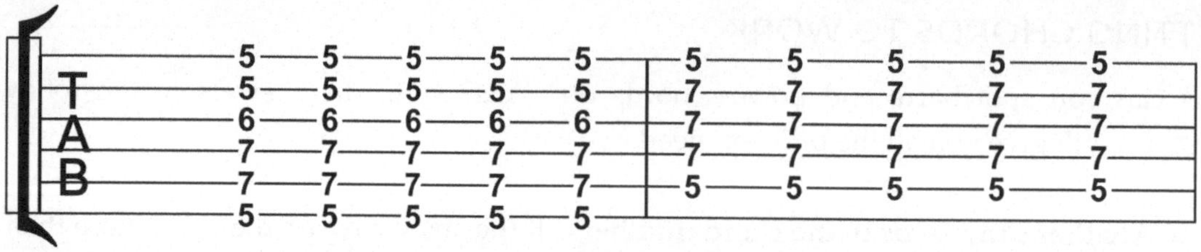

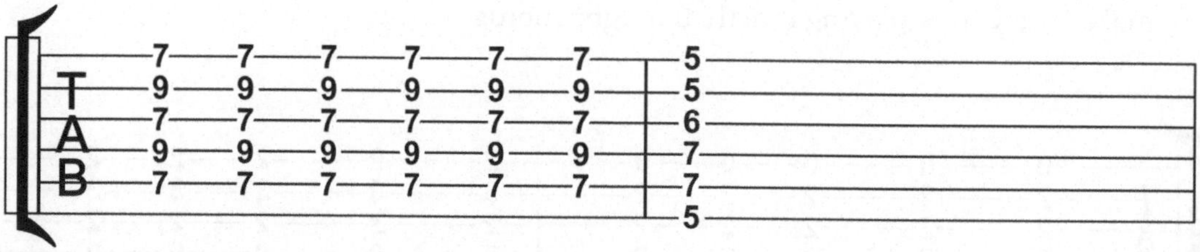

- **Do you have just two (or three) notes, and there are no zeros?** If the answer is yes, then you have a power chord. Pay attention to the number of the lowest note; it will give you the chord name.

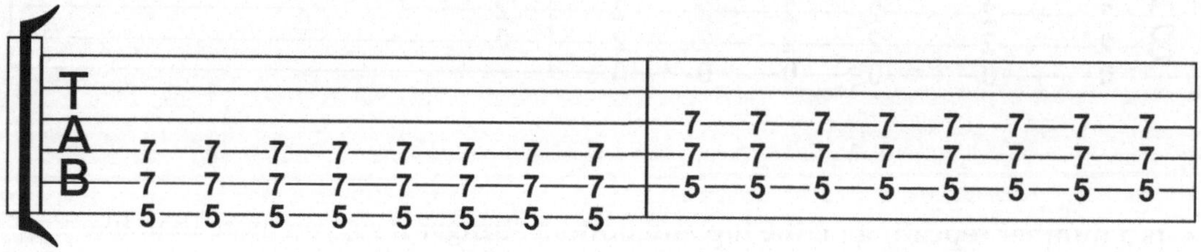

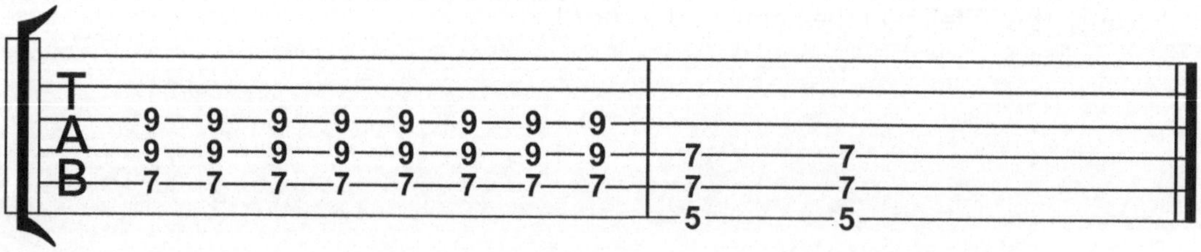

CHAPTER 4
RIFFS AND SOLOS IN TAB
LEARN THE MOVES THAT MAKE SONGS UNFORGETTABLE

I know, playing chords and figuring out your favorite songs is cool. But playing riffs and solos is even cooler! So, now that you're a TAB Wizard, it's time to start playing riffs and solos note by note.

This is what TABs are most useful for. They've saved me so many times when I got things wrong by ear. Trust me, you don't want to learn that lesson the hard way. I did, and it wasn't fun.

You might think that riffs and solos are just some notes played in a sequence, but getting both things right (the notes and the sequence) is super important.

Can you imagine changing the notes of AC/DC "Back in Black," for example? That will definitely get you booed off stage! TABs for riffs and solos can spare you from many epic fails and turn you into the player that everybody wants to be in a band with.

Believe me, I've been there, and it works like a charm.

Moving forward, step by step, you're becoming a better guitarist with each move. So let's keep going…

RIFFS, THE BACKBONE OF COUNTLESS HITS

What are riffs? Riffs are memorable, small pieces of music (or utterly complicated ones if you ask Jimmy Page) that are repeated. Moreover, a riff is a sequence of notes that is played following a rhythmic, percussive pattern.

Sounds complicated? Well, relax, because it's not. It's as simple as playing "Twinkle, Twinkle Little Star", but with more attitude and mojo.

To access the audio files for riff exercises in this section, head over to **playfirstnote.com/bonuses.**

Exercise 1

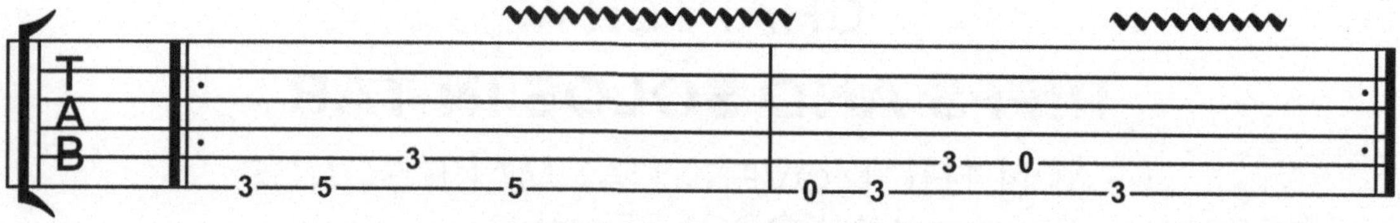

Let's get started with this simple riff that's played on the bottom two strings. It's meant to sound heavy and can be repeated to create a loop. If you happen to have an electric guitar and can add some distortion, do it; you'll be in riffing heaven!

You'll notice the wavy line extending from the final note of each bar. As you might recall from earlier in the book, when I went through the meaning of every TAB symbol, it shows that you need to add vibrato to those two notes.

Exercise 2

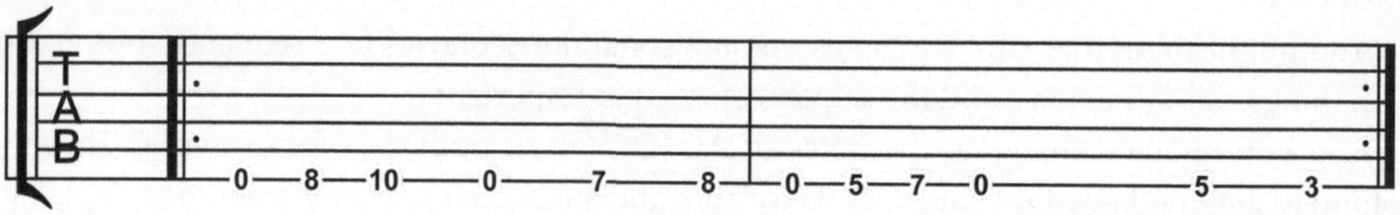

This is another exercise played on the low E string. It sounds great when distorted, but also sounds good when played clean. The key is to pay close attention to the note sequence, including the open string.

It's the open E that gives the riff its percussiveness, so take your time to get the right groove.

Exercise 3